Terri:

It's been so
great getting to know
and your family.

I hope you find something
book useful.

Be safe out there.

[signature]

7-11-15

**What Others Are Saying about Matthew Dubin
and *Maximizing Your Injury Claim***

"I have had the opportunity to act as a mediator on a significant number of cases handled by Matt Dubin. He prepares every case as if it will proceed to trial, which allows him to maximize the value of his clients' cases. In my experience, Mr. Dubin consistently obtains top tier resolutions for his clients."

— Keith Kubik, Mediation attorney, Kirkland, WA

"Filled with honest, straightforward advice, this powerful and invaluable resource demystifies 'scary' concepts of the insurance claim process in a way anyone can grasp. It arms you with information necessary to take the 'right' steps after (or before) an accident."

— Susan Friedmann, CSP, international best-selling author of *Riches in Niches: How to Make it BIG in a small Market*

"Matthew D. Dubin champions the rights of the wrongfully injured men and women in his community. He takes the personal time and care to understand the unique situation of every client. He honors clients devastated by personal injuries by aggressively pursuing full damages and visiting clients in the hospital and at home. I lend Matthew D. Dubin my personal endorsement."

— Howard Spiva, Personal injury lawyer, Savannah, GA

"Matt is an honest and hardworking lawyer who really puts his client's interests first. If you want to understand insurance coverage and the personal injury claims process, then start by reading this book. And if you've been hurt, Matt is the man to call."

— Kenneth Hardison, Social Security Disability lawyer,
North Myrtle Beach, SC

"If you need an attorney, I highly recommend going with the Law Offices of Matthew Dubin. All of the staff are very polite, professional, courteous, and downright friendly. They took care of everything. All I had to do was focus on getting better. They kept me informed every step of the way. It was an absolutely amazing experience."

— Cordelia Skorupa, Personal injury client

"Matt Dubin knows personal injury claims. He gets good results for his clients and his office staff is really nice. With this book, Matt offers an essential guide to insurance coverage and the personal injury claims process. If you want to protect your family from the potentially devastating consequences of an unexpected injury, you must read this book."

— Ryan Sargent, Personal injury lawyer, San Diego, CA

"Matt is a terrific attorney. He's a strong advocate for his clients, and they are lucky to have him."

— Vivi Vanderslice, Personal injury lawyer, Seattle, WA

"I have had the pleasure of working with Matt for a couple of years now, and I know that Matt is deeply committed to providing ever better legal services to his clients. I strongly endorse Matt to help anyone who has been injured and who needs an experienced, caring lawyer who can get the best possible results from the insurance company."

— Frances Jackson, Social Security Disability lawyer, Portland, ME

"Matt Dubin handled an auto accident case for me from 2009 until 2011. He was wonderful. He always kept me in the loop with what was going on in my case, but he did all the work himself. I didn't have to do anything except show up when I had appointments with him. I had no worries about my case at all after I put it in his hands. Matt is honest, trustworthy, skilled, personable, and fights for what is fair. He refused to take a lower offer than what was fair in my case, and he kept fighting for what was fair to me (and got it). We didn't even have to take it to court. I would recommend the Law Offices of Matthew D. Dubin to anyone."

— June Smith, Personal injury client

"If you drive, or if you care about someone who does, you must read this book. It will give you all the information you need to understand the complexities and nuances of a personal injury claim, and it will help you protect your family in the event of an injury. Matt is a great lawyer who deeply cares about his clients and getting them justice. His knowledge and compassion shine through in this amazing book."

— Patrick Snow, Best-Selling Author of
Creating Your Own Destiny and *Boy Entrepreneur*

"I have been working on several projects with Matt over the past year. His tenacity and attention to detail are unparalleled. He is my go to personal injury lawyer in Seattle, WA."

— John Page, Personal injury lawyer, Kirkwood, MO

"My three-year-old son had a traumatic finger amputation, and the property owner did not want to take responsibility. I called one lawyer, and he wouldn't take my case. Thank God for that because Matt Dubin did. He and his staff were great. They put me at ease and were very compassionate. They worked hard, and I feel my son got a reasonable settlement. Thank you so much!"

— Chantil Cripps, Mother of an injured child and personal injury client

"Matt Dubin and his entire staff uphold the highest principle of the legal profession in placing the individual client first. Matt himself sets the standard in professional excellence. His willingness to accept the challenges and responsibilities inherent in complex litigation and his talent have led me to refer cases, particularly automobile accident and workplace injury cases, to his firm. Matt Dubin and his firm are committed to investing the time and resources required to represent fully every client's case through the successive stages of investigation, preparation, and trial so each client receives what is just and reasonable. My patients regularly report that the service they receive from the Law Office of Matt Dubin is second to none!"

— James A. Devine, Chiropractor, Seattle, WA

"I was very fortunate to come across Matt Dubin's office. When you're banged up physically and emotionally, looking for an attorney is a daunting thing to do. However, after meeting with him and his staff, I felt so much at ease. I think what drew me to them initially was the statement on their website: 'Like a mother bear with her cubs, our Seattle personal injury lawyers are compassionate toward the injury victims they represent....' How true."

— Ana Wells, Personal injury client

"Matt Dubin has distilled the knowledge and experience of twenty years practicing personal injury law into this book. It is essential reading for anyone who wants to know what to do after a car wreck or other injury."

— Seth Bader, Workers Compensation attorney, Atlanta, GA

"Matt is an excellent attorney who has exceptional legal skills. He easily connects with people on a very personal level. Matt has that rare ability to leverage his knowledge, skills, and personality to achieve maximum results."

— Stephen Brooks, Personal injury lawyer, Winter Haven, FL

"I was in two accidents five years ago. My mom was actually the one to find Matt's office, and when we met with him, I was impressed with his knowledge and his confidence in taking on my case. His office was informative when I had questions, and the staff always made sure I understood the answers. They took care of talking to the insurance companies and health providers, and I had an extensive list! When I was stressed trying to get healthy, they took the stress off of me and my family. Even as my case dragged along, Matt never lost faith in my claim and the strength of my case against the insurance companies. He was always supportive and fought for me and what I needed."

— Marie Eisaman, Personal injury client

"Odds are that everyone will be in an auto accident during his lifetime, so *Maximizing Your Injury Claim* is a must-read for everyone. Let Matt Dubin walk you through everything from the many preventive measures you can take before the accident to what you can do to get the best settlement possible, and if need be, prepare for your day in court with the outcome you deserve. In the end, the money you can save, the assets you will protect, and the compensation you may receive all make this book priceless."

— Tyler R. Tichelaar, Ph.D., and award-winning author of *The Best Place* and *Arthur's Legacy*

"The insurance companies don't want you to know your rights. Matt Dubin does. If you want to know your rights and make sure the insurance companies can't take advantage of you, read this book."

— Gary Massey, Personal injury lawyer, Chattanooga, TN

"I've known Matt Dubin for seven years on a professional level and have come to call him 'THE TEDDY BEAR WITH TEETH.' He's a teddy bear with you, but wait till you see him in court—whew! The fangs come out, and he slices and dices whoever is on the other side of the room.... I've seen him chew people up in court and not blink an eye about it. I guess the thing I like most about Matt as a lawyer is that he actually does listen to his clientele and returns their phone calls. Since he isn't in a hundred lawyer practice, he can offer the personalized, one-on-one care that most cases need. Matt specializes in personal injury and medical liability issues, and not much else, but he's the best at them, and I would have no problem referring my friends and relatives to him without question."

— Peter Carr, Chiropractor, Seattle, WA

"I am from Alaska and was in an auto accident a few years back in Las Vegas, Nevada in a rental car. First advice, take out the insurance the rental company offers because it does pay off in the end. Second piece of advice, choose Matt Dubin to represent you. He will do everything to make sure you get the settlement you deserve. He believed in me and he knew I had a solid case. He has always been fair and upfront with me. Thanks, Matt."

— Barbie Svenson, Personal injury client

"Mr. Dubin goes the extra mile to make sure his clients are taken care of and treated well. I'm impressed with his professional manner and love of his clients."

— Lawrence Pew, Bankruptcy attorney, Mesa, AZ

"Matt Dubin and his entire staff treated us like family from day one. My husband had been in a four car pile-up on I-5 heading south into Seattle. There was no doubt he was injured, but he was in such pain it was hard for him to travel any distance. Matt took the time to come to our home instead of us having to come to him. We knew right away he was the right choice. His staff is customer-focused, efficient, and always available. Being injured at the fault of someone else is never an easy process, but then add in pending litigation, it is enough to drive you crazy. Matt and his staff took everything out of our hands so we felt no added stress. To me, they are the only personal injury attorneys worth hiring in Washington State."

— Kearsten Weeks, Personal injury client

"After my car accident, I needed to get a lot of treatment from different providers on my road to recovery. When my insurance company got nasty about my bills, I found Matt. He encouraged me to concentrate on getting better and leave the rest to him. So happy I did! Matt and his staff were great at settling my case."

— Diane Red, Personal injury client

"Matt Dubin and his staff call you back quickly and help with everything they can, and they don't leave you hanging to face the insurance company alone no matter what! Now that my fiancée is dealing with an accident and Matt is representing her, we have found out how important it is to have a lawyer with heart."

— David Alexanderson, Personal injury client

"I highly recommend Matt Dubin for his exceptional expertise and professionalism. I am very impressed with his explanation of the law and his advice on how to handle my situation. I've really enjoyed working with Matt and his staff. They are easy to get a hold of and easy to talk to. They work quickly, efficiently, and courteously. I will definitely recommend his firm to anyone looking for a good lawyer."

— Lindi Mondavi, Personal injury client

"Matt is approachable and can put someone at ease quite naturally. He is professional and reliable, and his staff is always well-informed about his case load. Matt won two cases for me, and in each instance, he communicated regularly, and he was honest about what I should or shouldn't expect. He assisted me in making decisions that weren't always easy, and through it all, he supported my choices. I am forever grateful."

— Eliane Follaca, Personal injury client

"We've used the services of Matthew Dubin's office in two separate injury cases, and the results couldn't have been any better. He was extremely patient with our situations, and he always advised us about what would be in our best interests—rather than pushing to settle the cases sooner than necessary. In both instances, we were able to secure very generous, but fair outcomes. We would definitely recommend Mr. Dubin's office to other individuals who are facing a personal injury case, and we plan to use Matthew for any future issues that arise for our family."

— Katie Seger, Personal injury client

"I have known Mr. Dubin for three years now, inside and outside the legal community, and I consider his zealous commitment to representing his clients to be superb. I have learned many creative strategies for protecting a client's rights from Matt, and I am confident that he uses that creativity for his clients' benefit beyond what even I know. I consider him to be a dedicated, trustworthy friend and colleague and would not hesitate to recommend him to an injured victim seeking justice."

— Paul Veillon, Personal injury lawyer, Seattle, WA

"I was referred to Matt by my friend and the passenger in a car accident. He was very efficient in settling the case for my friend. I was attempting to settle a very difficult case on my own with the insurance company, which was a bad decision on my part. I had already been writing letters and such, and when I needed to hire a lawyer, Matt stepped right in and is still on the case to settle my claim. I trust his judgment because he did not kick me to the curb when I had already been in the mix with this bullheaded insurance company."

— Tovia Bradley, Personal injury client

"I couldn't have asked for a nicer, more accepting, and compassionate, yet competent team of people to help me through a very tough time, especially in the beginning. I felt safe in my gut immediately. Matt and his staff provided me with detailed explanations and gave me a clear understanding of the big picture. They gave me the knowledge and time to choose wisely, and they got me a fair and honest outcome."

— Jennifer Bragg, Personal injury client

"After twenty-five years of fishing in Alaska, I suffered a career-ending accident due to a major airline's failure to de-ice its tarmac properly. After arriving back in Seattle, I went through hand surgery, which changed my whole career and life. The airline refused to accept responsibility until Matt Dubin took on my case. After Matt sued the airline and showed them he was serious about going to trial, it finally agreed to negotiate. After a difficult mediation, I received a large settlement for the loss of my career and the loss of full use of my hand. Thanks to Matt, I've been able to start my own business, become engaged, and begin a new start on life. Thank you, Matt, for taking the worst time of my life and giving me a chance to create a new and better future for myself and my new wife."

— Larry Johnson, Personal injury client

"This book is filled with common-sense wisdom about personal injury claims without any confusing legalese. You could learn more about the basics of personal injury law from reading this book than from sitting through a whole year of law school."

— Jodilyn Gilleland, First-year law student

A COMPASSIONATE GUIDE FOR VICTIMS OF PERSONAL INJURY

MAXIMIZING
YOUR INJURY CLAIM

SIMPLE STEPS TO PROTECT
YOUR FAMILY AFTER AN ACCIDENT

MATTHEW D. DUBIN

A NATIONAL TRIAL LAWYERS TOP 100 LAWYER

AVIVA
PUBLISHING
New York

MAXIMIZING YOUR INJURY CLAIM
SIMPLE STEPS TO PROTECT YOUR FAMILY AFTER AN ACCIDENT

Published by:
Aviva Publishing
Lake Placid, NY
(518) 523-1320 www.AvivaPubs.com

Matthew D. Dubin
Telephone: (206) 720-1501
Email: matt@dubinlawoffice.com
www.DubinLawOffice.com, www.MaximizingYourInjuryClaim.com

ISBN: 9781943164127

Library of Congress Control Number: 2015906137

Editor: Tyler Tichelaar
Cover Designer: NicoleGabriel, www.AngelDogProductions.com
Book Layout: NicoleGabriel, www.AngelDogProductions.com

Every attempt has been made to source properly all quotes.

Printed in the United States of America

First Edition

12 10 9 8 7 6 5 4 3 2 1

For Abraham

May you grow up with a deep understanding of your rights and the strength always to stand up for what is right, even against seemingly insurmountable odds.

ACKNOWLEDGMENTS

So many people have helped set the course of my life and led me to a career advocating for the rights of the injured. Among them, I would like to thank the following:

First, my mom, Patricia Dubin, and my sister, Melissa Falk, who taught me that there's nothing more important or more worthy of protection than family.

I would like to thank a couple of teachers who inspired me to be a better person. Marty Cohen, my social studies teacher at Felix Festa Middle School, who taught me that real life events can be more interesting than any fiction, and that one person can make a big difference. And Dr. Sam Draper, who taught me that with hard work and dedication, there is no limit to what a person can achieve.

Thank you to Eugene N. Bolin, Jr., who gave me my first job as an attorney and introduced me to personal injury law. Your dedication and enthusiasm for helping victims of negligence persuaded me to follow this path.

Thank you to Rebecca C. LaLiberte, whose commitment to protecting the rights of the injured matches my own. Your passion for justice and your desire to improve yourself inspire me on a daily basis.

Special thanks to Catherine Rosales, Mary Campbell, Martha Muldowney, Kelsey Christianson, Angela Gilleland, Lindsey Golden, and all of the young people who have worked at the Law Offices of Matthew D. Dubin over the years. Watching you discover the intricacies of personal injury law has always kept it fresh and exciting for me.

I am deeply grateful to Ken Hardison, Howard Spiva, Garry Salomon, and Patrick Snow for inspiring me to write this book and for showing me how to get it done.

Thanks to Tyler Tichelaar, who assisted me in the final editing of this book, and to Nicole Gabriel, who helped with the cover design.

I want to thank all of my past and current clients. It has been a great honor and a privilege to serve you and your families. I wish you nothing but the best, and I hope you never need my help again.

Finally, I thank my wife, Elizabeth, and my son, Abraham, who have always supported me, even when it meant nights and weekends away from home while I learned the important lessons contained in this book. Without your love and encouragement, I would not be half the man I am today.

Important Notices

This book is designed to give you general information regarding personal injury claims and lawsuits. It is not intended to give you personalized legal advice. While the general principles of personal injury law described in this book are applicable everywhere, the specific laws of each state differ. The area of law commonly called "tort law," which provides for awards of money damages for injuries resulting from another's breach of duty or negligence, is extremely complex. In fact, few lawyers have sufficient medical or courtroom training and experience even to venture into handling these cases.

Nothing in this book should be construed as specific legal advice since all cases are fact sensitive and unique. In order for lawyers to give legal advice, you must consult with them directly. While circumstances can vary, most commonly you will want to consult with an attorney licensed to practice in the state where your injury took place. If you decide to pursue your claim and a lawyer expressly decides to accept your case, you may "retain" him or her as your legal counsel. You do this by entering into an agreement, which in Washington State where I practice, must be in writing.

Accordingly, do not rely solely upon the contents of this book in making your decisions. Due to changes in the law, either through court decisions or by legislation, it is important that you consult with a competent and experienced personal injury lawyer before making any decisions.

This book is not intended to serve as a "do it yourself" manual to resolving your own personal injury claim. Experienced lawyers will certainly protect your interests and add significant value to any claim. In fact, few personal injury lawyers, myself included, would even consider representing themselves if injured in an accident.

This book is not intended to interfere with any legal relationship you may now have. If counsel already represents you, this book may raise and answer certain questions you may have. Please discuss these questions with your current lawyer. Each personal injury law firm practices law differently. If you are having a problem with your lawyer, meet with him or her and try to discuss the issues and work things out. If you lose confidence in your lawyer, you certainly can change counsel; however, this should only be done as a last resort.

CONTENTS

INTRODUCTION
PROTECTING YOUR FAMILY

If you were recently injured in an accident, you've probably already made one or more mistakes that could fatally harm your claim. Did you say the wrong thing at the scene of the accident? Did you fail to get the contact information for witnesses? Did you fail to get photos of the accident scene and the damages? Did you speak to the insurance company? Did you sign any documents? The fact is most people have no idea what to do after an accident. You don't know what your rights are or how to protect them. The insurance companies won't tell you what your rights are. To the contrary, they will make every effort to persuade you to give up your rights in exchange for a quick and cheap settlement. You are up against an industry whose primary objective is to pay you less than your claim is worth, or to pay you nothing at all if it can get away with it. Insurance companies have been doing this for a long time, and they are very good at it.

Are you overwhelmed by your injuries, medical appointments, and the demands of the insurance companies? Are you worried that you might be saying too much? Do you wonder whether you should have signed that form you just placed in the mail? Are you concerned that your insurance company or the other driver's insurance company might be taking advantage of you? Have you considered that you might not make a full recovery? Will you be able to provide for your family? Do you just want to return your life to the way it was before your accident?

I know exactly what you are going through. I've been there myself. I know what it's like to lay awake at night, unable to find a comfortable position and worrying how the bills will be paid. I know what it's like to have pain shooting down your leg and wondering whether it will ever go away. I know what it's like to have to show up for work despite the pain, and then to fill every free moment with doctor appointments, physical therapy, and home exercises. I know how the injury can affect not just you, but your whole family. The burden of an injury can be overwhelming, and the uncertainty of your recovery can be terrifying. It's okay to feel that way. I know how to get through it, and I want to help you.

In this book, you will learn all about personal injury claims, from before the accident happens until the end of trial (if trial becomes necessary). You will learn all about auto insurance coverage, and you will be given concrete steps you can take right now to protect your family in the event of an accident. You will learn about what happens at the scene of an accident, including the steps you must always take to optimize your claim and the things you should never do. In this book, you will learn how to decide whether you need a lawyer and how to choose the right lawyer for yourself and your family. You will learn about your rights and what you should expect after you hire a lawyer. You will learn simple steps you can take to increase the payment you receive for your damaged or totaled vehicle. You will learn about the dangers of social media and how to avoid sabotaging your claim on Facebook. You will learn about a variety of options available to make sure you get all of the medical treatment you need and that your bills get paid.

Sometimes, a claim can be settled, but sometimes, a lawsuit has to be filed to get you a fair recovery. In this book, you will learn about alternatives to trial, such as mediation and arbitration, and you will understand the factors that determine when it is best to settle and when it is best to file a lawsuit. You will learn about what happens after a lawsuit is filed, including the discovery period when each side gets to learn what the other knows. You will learn what happens at a real trial and how it is different from what you've seen on TV. Finally, you will learn how you get your money at the conclusion of the case, and what happens after your claim is closed.

This book contains true stories. Some are about me, but some are about my clients. Where I am describing clients' experiences, I have changed the names and some facts to preserve confidentiality, but the essence of the stories remains very real, and the stories have many essential lessons to teach us.

This book can be read from front to back, but it can also be used as a reference again and again. If you have a question about how to get your medical bills paid, you can go straight to that chapter. If you need help finding the right lawyer, go right to that section. Through-out the book, I have inserted questions and blank lines. I encourage you to use these spaces to help you clarify what is important to you and what specific steps you can take to protect yourself and your family in the event of an accident.

As I've stated above, I know what you are going through because I've been there myself. In 2002, I was injured in a rear-end car accident, and I went through over three years of treatment. I had an orthopedist who was ready to perform surgery on my lower back, but I opted for a more conservative course of treatment, and I eventually recovered. This experience certainly gives me empathy and understanding for what my clients are going through, but empathy alone will not get you through this process; you also need to know the ins and outs of the legal system. I received a B.A. in history from Yale University in 1990. After graduation, I worked for two years in a large litigation firm in New York City. At that job, I began to understand the intricacies of preparing a case for trial. I attended law school at the University of Washington where I obtained my J.D. in 1995. I was admitted to the bar that summer, and I've been representing injured people ever since. In the years since then, I've argued hundreds of cases and obtained recoveries for thousands of families. I have earned the highest possible ratings from several professional associations for both legal ability and ethical standards, and I have been named a Top 100 Trial Lawyer by the National Trial Lawyers and by the American Society of Legal Advocates. But more important to me than any of these accolades are the hundreds of reviews and testimonials I've received from my clients. It is my professional mission to educate people on their rights following an accident, to protect injured people and their families, and to build lasting relationships with my clients. No matter the size of a case, if I can accomplish those goals, I feel my job has been done, and I go home from the office feeling good about myself and what I do.

I understand why you haven't researched your rights or called a lawyer yet. You're already dealing with an injury on top of your job and your family. Why add to the hassle by having to find a lawyer, or even worse, trying to be your own lawyer. You're worried about the bad karma of making a claim against another person who probably just had a careless moment of inattention. You don't have time. You don't have any idea how to find the right lawyer. You might be worried about the cost of an attorney. Simply put, you are overwhelmed by the whole process, and you wish it would just go away. It's okay to feel that way. It's normal. Almost all of my clients have had one or more of these apprehensions. Together, we can address all of your concerns and give you more time and energy to get your life back to normal. I've got your back, and we can get through this together.

I want to be your advisor, your coach, your advocate, and your partner in this process. I want to create a protective bubble in which you can focus on recovering from your injuries and caring for your family. I want to be the shoulder you can rest your head on when you are overwhelmed by the whole process. I want to make sure your rights are protected and make sure you get what is owed to you. Let's lock arms and together take on the insurance industry that is determined to deny you and your family what you deserve.

Are you ready to begin? Are you ready to let go of the burden and the uncertainty and to let me be your guide through this process? Are you ready to return your attention to your recovery, your family, and your work? Are you ready to take all of the steps necessary to make sure you get a full and fair recovery for your claim? If so, let's begin this journey together.

Matthew D. Dubin

CHAPTER 1

ACTING NOW

Change your life today.
Don't gamble on the future, act now, without delay.

— Simone de Beauvoir

Ideally, you are reading this book *before* you, or your loved ones, have been injured in an accident. The most important things you can do to protect yourself and your family from the consequences of such an accident take place before the accident ever happens. You can make sure you have the optimal insurance coverage, as will be discussed in more detail in Chapter 3. You can know what to do and say (and what not to do) at the scene of an accident, as will be discussed in Chapter 4. Arming yourself with this basic protection and knowledge prior to an accident will increase the likelihood that your claim will go smoothly and that you will get a fair recovery.

That being said, even if you've already been in an accident, there are things you can do *right now* to reduce the chances that your claim will be compromised, to protect yourself and your family from the stress and burden of dealing with the insurance company, to insure that you get the medical treatment you need, and to maximize your recovery at the end of the case.

After practicing personal injury law for twenty years, claims for injuries following car accidents and other kinds of mishaps have become routine for me. Mind you, routine is not the same as boring. For me, the cases aren't about the law; they're about the people. Every client is a new relationship—a new experience. Each client has something to teach me and, hopefully, something to learn from me as well. At the conclusion of my cases, my clients become part of my "extended family," and I hope they continue to think of me as their attorney as well as their friend.

What makes each case unique is the people and the particular facts and circumstances each of them has experienced. Although specific laws can vary greatly from state to state, the general principles of personal injury law are pretty much the same in every case. I have spent over twenty years learning and practicing the law of personal injury cases in the State of Washington, and I continue regularly to attend classes and seminars on new developments in Washington personal injury law.

Of course, every now and then, I am confronted with a new issue of law—one I haven't seen before. In cases like that, I know exactly where to go to find the right answer, and I know how to apply that answer to the facts of the case. Legal research, while not always exciting, can be very rewarding when you find the answer to a difficult question that swings a case your way.

After all these years, it's easy for me to assume that everyone knows the basics of personal injury law. However, that isn't even close to being true. Unless you work for an insurance company or a personal injury lawyer, you probably don't know the difference between liability, personal injury protection, and underinsured motorist coverage. You probably don't know what to do after an accident to improve your chances of making a full recovery or the things that could reduce or even destroy the value of your claim. And, frankly, why should you? If you haven't been in an accident, you probably haven't had any reason to think about personal injury claims, except when you hear about some big verdict on the news.

Over the years, new clients have come to my office with every kind of misconception and misunderstanding about personal injury cases. They simply have no idea how the insurance companies view these cases, what a lawyer does for them, or how the process works. I have found that one of my most important jobs as an attorney is to educate my clients on the realities of personal injury law and then to empower them with the knowledge and tools to use the legal system to achieve their goals.

My purpose in writing this book is to broaden that mission of educating my clients to helping the public at large understand the specifics of a personal injury claim. If one person learns the lessons in this book before he is in an accident, it was worth it. If one person calls her insurance company to make sure she has adequate PIP coverage, or knows what to do at the scene of an accident before it happens, I will have done my job.

The fact is that multiple factors are lined up against victims of car accidents and other personal injuries. The insurance industry and big corporations have been waging an aggressive campaign for more than twenty years to malign our civil justice system, and especially those who would use it to seek compensation for injuries. Sadly, this campaign has been relatively successful in creating a stigma around personal injury claims and the attorneys who represent injured claimants.

In order to overcome this bias, an injured person must do everything right in order to have the best chance of making a full recovery. That means making sure the right insurance coverage is in place before the accident, making sure you do and say the right things at the scene of the accident, and taking appropriate action after the accident. If you do these things, your chances of getting fair compensation for your injuries dramatically improve.

WILDERNESS CAMP

If you've been in an accident, what is the first thing you should do? Whom should you speak to and whom should you never speak to? Are there any documents you should sign? What kind of doctor should you see, and who will pay that doctor? Most importantly, if you aren't a lawyer, how on earth are you supposed to know the answers to these questions?

For most people, the aftermath of an injury is like entering a new world—an unknown wilderness. Without the proper equipment, preparation, and guidance, you could easily get lost in this wilderness. You could go down the wrong trail or eat the wrong plant with potentially disastrous consequences. But the wilderness isn't inherently bad—it's just unfamiliar. By arming yourself now with some basic knowledge about the anatomy of an injury claim, you will be in a position to protect yourself and your family when the need arises, even if the need is right now.

In the summer of 1980, at age eleven, I began to attend a wilderness summer camp in Harriman State Park in upstate New York. I returned to this camp annually for the next six years. At this camp, groups of kids would go on five-day adventures every week, and then we would return to camp for the weekends. We did backpacking, canoeing, bicycling, rock climbing, and other fun and challenging wilderness trips.

So what did I, an eleven-year-old boy from the suburbs, know about camping in the wilderness? Nothing. I literally knew nothing. I may have spent the night in my backyard in a tent, but that was the extent of my wilderness training. How could I possibly survive a week-long backpacking trip along the Appalachian Trail or a canoe trip down the Delaware River?

The answer, of course, is that I didn't do it alone.

The camp provided expert counselors, experienced in all of the skills necessary not just to survive, but to thrive in the wilderness. They taught us what equipment we would need and how to use it. They taught us what food we would need, and they helped us prepare it. In fact, a big part of every Sunday was dedicated to food preparation, and we would prepare an entire week's worth of meals and snacks, which we then carried on our backs.

But training and preparation were only part of the program. The counselors (of course) came with us on our adventures. We were, after all, only eleven or twelve years old, and we really had no wilderness experience. When we made poor decisions, the counselors helped us fix things. When we walked in the wrong plants and got poison ivy, they showed us how to treat it and how to avoid being exposed again. When we got lost, they pulled out a map and compass and showed us how to find our way back to safety. When our food was exposed to the elements and ruined, they made sure we had enough to eat and showed us how to pack the food for the next time so it would stay safe and dry.

After a few trips, we became pretty good at taking care of ourselves. Some of us even considered ourselves experts. But some unknown danger was always lurking around the next bend—a crumbling old building, dangerous rapids on the river, a poisonous snake, or a plain old broken arm. That's why, even though we felt like we were fully prepared for any situation, the counselors always stayed with us. They watched us, providing guidance whenever it would help, and bailing us out of difficult situations whenever they arose.

So, coming back to the aftermath of an accident, how do you know what to do? The answer is that you probably don't. There's no shame in that. You simply haven't had the training, experience, or coaching necessary to make the best judgments in the various situations likely to arise.

I challenge you to use the lines provided below to write the three most important things you believe you can do *right now* to protect yourself and your family from the consequences of an accident. What you write may depend on whether you've already been in an accident or not, but just write down three actions. Then, as you proceed through this book, I encourage you to revisit what you wrote and see whether you still agree that those were, in fact, the three most important things you could do.

1. _____
   _____
   _____
   _____

2. _____
   _____
   _____
   _____

3. _____
   _____
   _____
   _____

CHAPTER 2
UNDERSTANDING THE PERSONAL INJURY CLAIM

Nothing in life is to be feared, it is only to be understood.
Now is the time to understand more, so that we may fear less.

— Marie Curie

In the last chapter, we discussed things you can do right now to advance your injury claim. But what exactly is a personal injury claim? In this chapter, I'll tackle that question and try to provide an overview of the typical personal injury claim.

We've all heard the terms "Personal Injury," "Personal Injury Lawyer," and "Personal Injury Claim," but what do those terms really mean?

Technically, a "personal injury" is simply any injury to a person. Of course, not all injuries result in claims. When we refer to "personal injury claims," what we are really referring to is negligence claims. Negligence is the failure to exercise reasonable care. When a person is careless, and that carelessness results in an injury to someone else, a personal injury claim results.

The question of what constitutes "reasonable care" is complicated, and it is usually not clearly spelled out by the law. Even where there are specific rules, such as traffic laws, or construction safety codes, violation of those rules in Washington may only be considered by a jury as "evidence of negligence." Ultimately, it is up to the jury to determine whether a defendant exercised "reasonable care."

There is a wide range of personal injury claims, from medical malpractice (failure to exercise the minimum care that would be used by a reasonably careful doctor under the same or similar circumstances), to landowner liability (failure to correct or warn of an unreasonably dangerous condition on property), to auto accidents (failure to use reasonable care when driving). Countless other kinds of personal injury claims exist, such as dog bites, slip and falls, trip and falls, nursing home neglect, and many more.

Making things even more confusing, different rules apply to different defendants. For example, the "standard of care" for a bus driver may be higher than that applied to a person driving her own private car, and what is reasonable for an adult is different than what is reasonable for a child.

The common thread connecting all of these circumstances is that somebody, some person or corporation, failed to use reasonable care (a defendant), and as a result of that failure, some person (a plaintiff) suffered an injury.

Not all injuries result from negligence, and not all negligence causes injuries. Even when an injury is caused by someone's negligence, circumstances may prevent that injury from ever becoming a personal injury claim. Time limits exist for bringing a claim, and certain defendants are exempt from certain types of claims. In other circumstances, your claim may simply be too small to justify the expense and effort necessary to pursue it, or it may be complicated by your medical history.

If you have been injured, and you believe your injury was caused by another person's carelessness, the best way to know for sure whether you have a claim worth pursuing is to consult with an attorney experienced in handling personal injury claims.

THE TREATMENT PHASE

Before you can settle your claim, you need to know what it's worth. Before you can know what it's worth, you need to know how the injuries affect your life, how long your treatment lasts, and how much your bills are. Although there's no way to know those things until your treatment is finished, the liability insurer (the defendant's insurance company) will want to speak to you right away, and it will possibly offer you a settlement, before your treatment has concluded.

The fact is that you don't have to speak to the liability insurer, but it doesn't want you to know that. A claimant who doesn't know his rights can be more easily manipulated and taken advantage of. The following story illustrates the tactics that insurance companies will use to avoid paying fair settlements:

Alex Bland was crossing the street. Although it was a four-lane street and he was crossing mid-block, he had looked both ways and no traffic was approaching in either direction. As he was crossing, a pickup truck pulled out of a parking lot and turned left onto the roadway. The driver of the truck never looked to his left and drove right into Alex.

Alex was thrown from the impact. He used his arms to brace himself, and he suffered torn shoulders and a crushed lower leg. He was transported by ambulance to the hospital, where he underwent emergency surgery to reduce the swelling in his leg, which was cutting off circulation to his foot.

The next day, the claims adjuster called the hospital room, wanting to take a recorded statement. Alex was in extreme pain and was on high doses of narcotics, but the insurance company had no reservations about questioning him regarding the facts of the accident, his injuries, and his treatment.

Fortunately, Alex's wife, who was there with him at the time, had the sense to call me first. I advised her that he was under no obligation to give a statement at any time, but that he certainly should not speak to the insurance company under those circumstances. Alex's wife informed the adjuster that he was hiring me as his attorney. I advised the insurance company that I would make Alex available for a statement at an appropriate time. Two months later, once his recovery was well underway, I let the adjuster ask Alex questions about the accident.

A few weeks later, the insurance company offered its policy limits to settle Alex's claim. This was the best possible outcome. Alex accepted the policy limits and proceeded to make a claim against his own underinsured motorist policy.

It is possible that no harm would have come from Alex giving a recorded statement to the claims adjuster from his hospital bed while on pain medication, but you can be sure the insurance company wanted to blame the accident on him. If he had been pressured into giving a statement while woozy and disoriented, who knows what he might have said and how the adjuster could have used it against him?

You have NO OBLIGATION to speak to the liability insurance company until you are ready. If its representative tells you such a statement is required, *that person is lying*. If he threatens to "close the case," let him. It can be reopened at any time.

When you know your rights and obligations, you are far less likely to be manipulated by the insurance company.

Your treatment continues until you and your doctors agree that you are recovered, or that you have reached a state of "maximum medical improvement." Nobody else can decide when your treatment is finished—not the insurance company and not your lawyer.

Once you have completed the treatment phase, you are ready to move the case forward.

THE NEGOTIATION PHASE

While trial is sometimes necessary, it can be risky, expensive, and time-consuming. In most cases, it makes sense to explore the possibility of settlement first. This is done through demand and negotiation.

Your lawyer will gather all of the documents and information relevant to your claim. This includes photos, police reports, witness statements, employment records, medical bills and records, and anything else that supports your claim.

In addition to all of the documents, a good lawyer will make a real effort to understand you and your family and how you were all affected by your injuries. The greatest value of your claim comes not from your medical bills, but from the non-economic damages. An attorney who knows and understands you is in a much better position to persuade the insurance company that your case is different from the statistics on its computer screen. When we get the claims adjuster to view you as a real person and not just a claim number, we've already won half the battle.

Several years ago, I represented Earl Danbury, a small farmer living south of Seattle. His injuries were pretty straightforward. He had a bulging disc in his neck that required surgery and essentially prevented him from working. Following the surgery, Earl's doctor placed limitations on him that made it impossible for him to return to the active lifestyle he had enjoyed before the accident.

We could have simply presented the medical reports and bills, along with the extra expenses involved in keeping the farm running, but because we really knew Earl and how much working on the farm meant to him, we were able to add a whole additional dimension to his claim.

We weren't able to get Earl back into the fields, but we were able to get him a fair recovery that reflected the REAL value of his loss. After his settlement, Earl was able to sell his farm and retire comfortably.

Not all cases settle that easily. Some require outside assistance, such as professional mediation. Even with help, some cases simply can't settle. When the insurance company views the case so much differently than the plaintiff and his or her lawyer do, sometimes there's no choice but to file a lawsuit. But when your lawyer knows you not as a file, but as a real person with a life, a job, and a family, the chances of reaching a fair settlement are enhanced immensely.

THE LITIGATION PHASE

If you and your lawyer can't negotiate a settlement to your claim, the next step is to file a lawsuit. Filing a lawsuit does not necessarily mean you will end up in court. Negotiations can continue after you file, and often filing will be what it takes to prompt the insurance company to make a reasonable offer. After you've filed, you and your lawyer can try to settle your case with the assistance of a mediator, and you can bypass the jury system by arguing your claims to an arbitrator.

During this phase, an extensive exchange of information occurs between you and the insurance company lawyers. This is called discovery. During discovery, each side gets to ask written questions and interview witnesses under oath in depositions.

Finally, if the case has not settled, there is a trial. At the trial, your lawyer uses witnesses and exhibits to tell the story of your claim to a judge or jury. You will learn more about the trial in Chapter 21.

While most claims are resolved before a lawsuit ever needs to be filed, a good lawyer will always be prepared to file a lawsuit and to take your case all the way to trial if necessary.

CONCLUSION

A personal injury claim is not as simple as you might think. There are many nuances and many opportunities for you to make the wrong move. Getting an attorney early in the process can minimize the risk that you will do or say something wrong, and it can maximize your chances of getting a full recovery. But even before the injury takes place, there are things you can do to increase your odds of getting full compensation following an injury. The first thing, addressed in the next chapter, is to make sure you have adequate insurance coverage.

CHAPTER 3

OPTIMIZING YOUR INSURANCE COVERAGE

*Insurance is the only product that both the seller
and buyer hope is never actually used.*

— Unknown

In Chapter 2, we discussed the basic anatomy of a personal injury claim, from beginning to end. We discussed how knowing your rights and choosing a good attorney can make all the difference in getting you a fair recovery. Here in Chapter 3, we will discuss steps you can take *before* an accident that will provide additional security for you and your family. We will explain the different types of auto insurance available and how to decide which coverage is best for you.

Do you know what your auto insurance coverage is? Do you know how much your limits are? If you do, you're the exception. When I speak to groups and ask this question, usually less than 10 percent of the people raise their hands. The first step in optimizing your insurance coverage is to know what you already have.

Not all personal injury claims result from car accidents, but these accidents are by far the most common cause of injury claims. As a result, this book deals extensively with the topic of auto accidents and auto insurance. Every state has some requirement for auto insurance. Because of this requirement, nearly everyone has some kind of insurance. However, I am continually surprised by how little people actually know about auto insurance. This chapter breaks down auto insurance into its most common components, explains what each coverage does, and advises you on the essential coverage you should make sure you have to protect yourself and your family.

The most common types of insurance coverage are liability, uninsured or underinsured coverage, and personal injury protection (PIP). In addition, you can usually purchase comprehensive coverage, rental car coverage, roadside assistance, and many other options.

Let's take a look at each kind of coverage and see what it does and how it works:

LIABILITY COVERAGE

Liability is the only coverage required by law in the State of Washington. At the time this book was written, the law required every driver to carry a minimum of $25,000 per person and $50,000 per incident (25/50). Liability coverage protects you when you cause an accident by paying for the damages or injuries you cause, up to the amount of your limits.

Liability coverage does not completely shield you from personal liability. For example, if you have the minimum coverage and you cause someone to become paralyzed, that person can refuse to accept your insurance limits and sue you directly. As long as your insurance company offered to pay your limits, it is then likely off the hook for any judgment against you in excess of those limits. Because of this, it's a good idea to carry more liability insurance than your net worth. People with very high net worth are often advised to carry an umbrella liability policy, which provides an additional layer of liability coverage above and beyond their auto coverage.

Unfortunately, most people don't have very high limits of liability coverage, and in Washington, despite the law requiring insurance, nearly 20 percent of drivers have no insurance at all. When you are injured by another driver's negligence, it is that driver's liability coverage you will be seeking in your claim. In most cases, your recovery will be limited by the other driver's policy limits because he simply doesn't have any assets worth going after.

Here's a real-life example:

Sam and Carla Bronson and their four-year-old daughter, Ellie, were driving home in their minivan. A drunk driver speeding down the freeway rear-ended the family vehicle, causing it to lose control and spin into another car with a driver and a passenger. All three of the Bronsons were hurt. Sam broke his arm, Carla suffered neck and back injuries and a mild traumatic brain injury, and Ellie suffered some scrapes and bruises. The occupants of the other car were also hurt, each having neck and back injuries. Unfortunately, the guy who caused the accident had minimum coverage of $25,000 per person and $50,000 per accident. This limits the claims in two important ways. First, no one claimant can recover more than $25,000. Carla's medical bills alone were in excess of $25,000, but the policy limits protect the insurer from paying more than $25,000 per person. Second, the insurance company will not pay more than $50,000 total for the claims of all five injured people combined.

So what's an injured person to do? In this example, the person who caused the collision had no assets. Without some other source of insurance, the recovery could be limited to the liability insurance limits. Fortunately, my clients had purchased uninsured/underinsured motorist coverage (UM/UIM) with their own auto insurance. We will address that coverage next.

In summary, liability coverage protects your assets if you cause harm to someone else. It's a good idea to carry liability coverage in an amount equal to or in excess of your net worth. If you have a high net worth, it might be worthwhile to look into an umbrella liability policy in addition to your auto coverage.

UNINSURED/UNDERINSURED MOTORIST COVERAGE (UM/UIM)

While your liability coverage pays for the damages you cause, it does not do anything to help you when you are injured by someone else. Once that person's liability coverage is exhausted, or if he doesn't have insurance, you are out of luck unless you have purchased uninsured/underinsured coverage as part of your own auto insurance.

This type of coverage is specifically designed to pay for your damages when the person who caused the accident is uninsured or underinsured. This is not a no-fault coverage, so you still need to prove that the person who caused the accident was negligent, and that your injuries were caused by that negligence, and your insurance company will often fight you on that. But if you can prove those things, then the coverage is there to compensate you for your losses.

The interesting thing about UM/UIM coverage is that your insurance acts as if it is the liability insurance for the person who caused the accident. That means it will use all of the tactics the other driver's insurance would use—denying fault for the accident, blaming your injuries on something else, and arguing that your treatment was excessive. *Your insurance company has no loyalty to you*, even if you've been paying the same company monthly premiums for years. If you are asking it for money, you are its adversary, and it will aggressively work to minimize your recovery.

You are usually not allowed to purchase UM/UIM coverage with a higher limit than your liability coverage, which is another reason you should always have more than the minimum required by law. A limit of $25,000 may seem like a lot, but with a serious injury, you could have medical bills in excess of $25,000 within days. With so many uninsured and underinsured drivers on the road, you owe it to yourself and your family to make sure you are adequately covered. I recommend paying a little more for at least $100,000/$300,000 coverage for both liability and UM/UIM. This amount will be adequate to cover all but the most catastrophic claims, and it will protect you if you suffer a serious injury.

PERSONAL INJURY PROTECTION COVERAGE (PIP)

Where liability and UM/UIM require a showing of fault, which can often take months, or even years to establish, if you've been injured in an accident, you have medical bills that need to be paid now. PIP coverage addresses this problem. PIP is a no-fault medical payments coverage, which means you do not need to establish responsibility for causing the accident in order to get paid. Instead, you need only show that the treatment you are claiming was reasonable, medically necessary, and causally related to the collision, and the bills will be paid, up to the limits of your coverage.

Even if you were riding in someone else's car when you were hurt, if that person doesn't have PIP coverage, your PIP will cover you. Many insurance companies exclude coverage for injuries that take place while using mass transit, so if you frequently ride the bus, call your insurance company and make sure your medical bills will be covered if you are injured while riding a bus.

In a way, PIP coverage is like health insurance for injuries caused by an accident, only without deductibles, co-pays, preferred providers, etc. In Washington, the most common amounts of PIP coverage are $10,000 and $35,000. I strongly recommend at least the $35,000 level of coverage.

Following a motor vehicle collision, your PIP coverage is primary. That means your insurance company has the first obligation to pay your accident-related bills. Only after your coverage is exhausted or denied does your regular health insurance come into play.

Sometimes, during the course of your treatment, your insurance company will require you to attend an "independent" medical examination (IME). I usually refer to these as insurance medical examinations because all of the insurance companies routinely use the same few doctors for these examinations, and those doctors know where their bread is buttered. Those who don't say what the insurance companies want them to say don't keep getting this business for very long. As a result, IMEs often result in your auto insurance cutting off your PIP coverage. However, your insurance policy contains a duty of cooperation, and if you refuse to attend the IME, it will terminate your coverage anyway.

It's a very good idea to have an attorney involved if your insurance company is demanding an IME. An attorney can set limitations or guidelines on the examination, and he or she can even arrange to have a medical professional or paralegal attend the IME to document independently exactly what is said and done.

At the conclusion of your claim, your PIP carrier has a claim to be reimbursed for the payments it made. This claim is called subrogation. Because your recovery from the person who caused the accident includes all of your medical bills, part of this money has to go back to the insurance company that paid those bills. Fortunately for injured people in Washington, our Supreme Court has held that because the PIP insurer benefits from the lawyer's work, it must also pay its share of the lawyer's fee and costs. This insures that the injured person is only paying an attorney fee on the money he actually received and the insurance company pays a fee on the medical bills the attorney recovers for it.

Some people are worried about using their PIP coverage because they don't want to make a claim on their own insurance. Some of them are afraid their rates will go up. Others just don't think it's right that their company should have to pay for damages caused by someone else. As for the first concern, the criteria insurance companies use to make rate determinations are a mystery, but in general, your rates should not go up for an incident that was not your fault. Further, you have a duty under your insurance policy to report any accidents to your insurer, so you might as well get the benefit of the coverage you have paid for. Finally, when you make a recovery from the insurer of the person who caused the accident, your insurer will get paid back. We have insurance for a reason. If you are injured in an accident, you should use it.

OTHER COVERAGES

An insurance policy is nothing more than a contract between you and the insurance company. You are agreeing to pay your premium every month and to cooperate with the insurance company's investigation when a claim is made, and the company is agreeing to pay for certain losses. In theory, you could negotiate any kind of coverage, but a few standard ones are good to consider:

- **Comprehensive coverage** takes care of minor losses such as cracked windshields, minor dents or scratches, and damage to accessories such as windshield wipers.

- **Rental car coverage** pays for a rental car when your car has been damaged, is undriveable, or is in the shop getting repaired.

- **Roadside assistance coverage** is provided by many insurers, and it will provide you with a tow truck, a jump start, or a can of gas when you are stranded. I personally prefer AAA for this service, but you may be able to get the same or comparable service through your insurance company.

THE IN-LAWS

Everyone should know what his or her auto insurance coverage is and should check it frequently to make sure the coverage remains optimal for his or her family. This is also true for lawyers and their families.

I tend to talk about auto insurance—a lot. It's kind of what I do. So, finally, after hearing me talk about it for years, my father-in-law asked me to take a look at his declaration page during a family visit. What I found shocked me.

My in-laws had excellent liability coverage. If they ever hit someone else, that person would be well-covered. But their UM and PIP coverage was so low that they might as well not have had any coverage at all. I begged them—BEGGED THEM—to call their insurance company IMMEDIATELY and max out their UM and PIP coverage. They took my advice, and for a few extra dollars each month, they protected themselves.

Less than three months later, my father-in-law was seriously injured in an accident. He required multiple surgeries, and the bills were very high. Fortunately, he had the coverage he needed to make sure his bills were paid, and he was able to get a fair recovery even though the guy who hit him had low limits.

Now I'm begging you. Check your insurance now to make sure you have the best possible UM/UIM and PIP coverage. If you ever need it, you'll be glad you did.

DISASTER

If you don't have UM and PIP coverage and you are injured by an uninsured or underinsured driver, the results could be a disaster. That's exactly what happened to Sandy Fitzpatrick.

Sandy was riding her boyfriend's motorcycle to the store. The motorcycle had been in storage for six months and was not insured. Sandy also had no insurance of her own. But it was just a short ride to the store. What could possibly go wrong?

As Sandy was following her boyfriend down a main street, a teenage driver blew through a stop sign and drove right across her path. Sandy tried to stop, but she was unable to. Her bike hit the car and she was thrown over the car and onto the pavement. She suffered a severely broken pelvis and other major injuries. She spent more than a week in the hospital and more than a month in bed. It took her more than a year to recover fully, and even then, she had a permanent disability and was unable to get pregnant.

The kid who hit her was an unemployed eighteen year old living with his grandfather. He had $25,000 in liability insurance. That wasn't enough to cover even the first day of Sandy's medical bills. We hired a private investigator to run an asset check on the kid and his grandfather, but neither had any assets. We could take the kid to court and get a judgment against him, but realistically, Sandy would never see any of that money.

Ultimately, the kid took responsibility. We agreed to take the $25,000 insurance limits and an additional $25,000 to be paid over five years. Unfortunately, the kid soon defaulted and we referred the case to a collection specialist to try to get something for Sandy. Bills remained unpaid, and Sandy never got any compensation for the pain, disability, and dramatic effect the injury had on her life.

Imagine how much different it could have been if Sandy had Personal Injury Protection and Underinsured Motorist Coverage. Her bills would have been promptly paid. She would have been compensated for the impact on her life. The money can never undo the injury, but at least she would have had a foundation upon which to start rebuilding her life.

CONCLUSION

When it comes to your auto insurance coverage, you can't rely on an agent to tell you what you need. Do your homework, know what coverage is available, and make sure you and your family are protected from the most likely risks. Don't try to save a few bucks by waiving PIP coverage. It is so important to make sure that you can get the medical treatment you need following an accident with the minimum delay and hassle. Maximize your uninsured/underinsured motorist coverage. Too many uninsured drivers are out there for you to for you to gamble by having inadequate coverage.

- Using the list below, check your own auto insurance coverage now to make sure it is adequate to protect you and your family in the event of a catastrophic car wreck. If it is not, call your insurance company now and increase your coverage. If you have any questions about what kind of coverage you should get, call a personal injury attorney and ask for advice.

- Liability – You should have an amount equal to or greater than your net worth. Because you cannot get UM/UIM coverage in excess of your liability coverage, I recommend everyone get at least $100,000 per person/$300,000 per incident (100/300).

- UM/UIM – You should have as much as you can afford, but no less than 100/300.

- PIP – Again, as much as you can afford, but at least get some. I recommend at least $35,000.

- Additional coverages to consider include comprehensive, rental car coverage, and roadside assistance coverage.

CHAPTER 4

KNOWING WHAT TO DO (AND NOT DO) AT THE SCENE OF AN ACCIDENT

Risk comes from not knowing what you're doing.

— Warren Buffett

Because most personal injury claims result from motor vehicle collisions, this book deals primarily with that topic. It should be noted that although I sometimes use the term "accident," I prefer to refer to these events as incidents, collisions, or wrecks. The reason is that sometimes "accidents" just happen, but most motor vehicle collisions are not "accidents." They result from someone doing something wrong. Carelessness, inattention, and distracted or drunk driving are not accidents. Instead, they are a failure to exercise reasonable care in the operation of a powerful and dangerous machine, which often results in serious injuries to an unsuspecting person sharing the road.

What you do in the minutes and hours following a motor vehicle collision can have a dramatic effect on how your personal injury claim goes. By following a few basic steps, you can make sure you give yourself the best possible chance to make a recovery for your injuries. For organizational purposes, I'll divide these steps into two categories: what to do at the scene, and what not to do at the scene.

THE BACKEST

Would you know what to do in an emergency situation? Do you act differently in different situations? What would you do if a family member fell out of your car?

When I was a kid, we had a station wagon. It had a front seat, a back seat, and what my sister and I called "the backest." Back in those days, people rarely used seat belts, and kids were often free to move around the car. My sister and I used to fight over who got to ride in the backest.

One day—I honestly don't remember how old I was, but I couldn't have been older than five—as we were making a turn, the rear hatch of the car opened and my sister fell out onto the pavement in the middle of the intersection.

Can you imagine the shock and terror my parents must have felt? Now imagine that the hatch didn't just open on its own, but that it was caused by a collision. Do you think a parent would be thinking rationally? Do you think he or she would take the time to identify witnesses or take photos? Do you think the parent would have any idea what to do?

In the case of my sister, she was fine, and we left the scene without consequence, but what if the facts had been a little different? Knowing what to do at the scene of a collision could be the difference between making a recovery and getting nothing.

WHAT TO DO AT THE SCENE

Stay safe. You've already been hurt and your car is damaged. The last thing you need is to get hit or hurt again. Leave the car where the incident occurred unless it is unsafe to do so. This will allow the police to document the facts of the accident properly and accurately. If you cannot leave your car at the scene of the accident, pull safely to the side of the road and remain in your vehicle. Additional injuries can occur if proper precautions are not taken.

Call the police. You should contact emergency personnel immediately after a collision. Even if you don't think you are seriously hurt, you should always call the police. The police will take statements and will preserve evidence and the identities of witnesses. If the police refuse to come out because the accident was in a private parking lot or there were no apparent injuries, get the insurance information, address, and phone number from the other driver, as well as contact information for any witnesses. If possible, take a picture of the other driver's license and insurance card.

Take as many pictures as you can. These days, nearly everyone has a phone with a camera. You should photograph the damage to all of the vehicles involved, the overall scene, and any visible injuries. If bruising or other injuries become apparent later, you should photograph those as well. Take as many pictures as you can from different angles. In motor vehicle collisions and the claims that follow, a picture really can be worth a thousand words.

Promptly seek medical treatment. If you are offered an ambulance or aid car from the scene, take it. If you are not offered an ambulance, or if you turn it down for some reason, you should go to the emergency room and get checked out. Even if you think you're okay, the adrenaline is flowing and you could have injuries you aren't even aware of yet. An examination at the emergency room will rule out any potentially life-threatening injuries, and it will provide you with guidelines for your future doctor visits.

If you choose not to go to the emergency room, you should, at a minimum, see your primary care physician as soon as possible following the collision, regardless of whether you consider your injuries serious or minor. Your doctor will document your complaints, record any objective indications of injury, and prescribe pain medications or muscle relaxants if necessary. Your doctor is also the best person to prescribe a treatment plan, which might include physical therapy, chiropractic, massage, acupuncture, or additional diagnostic testing.

Report the incident to your insurance company. It is not necessary to call your insurance company from the scene of the collision, but many insurance companies do require that you report an incident promptly after it happens. Many people believe that if the accident wasn't their fault, they have no obligation to report it to their insurance company, but that's simply not true. Failing to report it to your insurance company could make it much more difficult later for you to get the benefits you've paid for.

Many people worry that reporting an incident to their insurance company will result in their premiums going up. The bottom line is this: nobody can tell you exactly when or why your premiums might go up. Insurance companies operate in ways that to anyone outside the insurance industry seem mysterious and without reason. But in general, if the incident was not your fault, your premiums should not go up. You've paid for insurance coverage for all these years, and now is the time to use it. Don't be shy about it. If you are entitled to benefits, you need to be claiming them. Your insurance company wouldn't hesitate to get extra money from you. You need to approach this situation the same way.

If you do these simple things at the scene of the collision, you will be positioned to advance your personal injury claim with the least amount of hassle, and you will have the maximum information necessary to help a qualified personal injury attorney get you the best possible recovery, either through negotiation, arbitration, or trial.

WHAT NOT TO DO AT THE SCENE

Above were the things you should do at the scene of the accident, or shortly after you leave the scene. There are also things you should definitely NOT do at the scene. Avoiding these common mistakes will increase the chances that you will be safe and protected and that your injury claim will not be compromised.

Don't leave the scene. Even if the damage seems minor and nobody seems to be hurt, it's never okay just to leave the scene of an auto accident. No matter how minor it was, you are required to stop, make sure there are no injuries, exchange insurance information, and report the incident to law enforcement. The police may not come to the scene, but you should still report it.

It may be that you are the one who was hurt, and you haven't even realized it due to the shock of the accident and the adrenaline in your system. Even if you aren't hurt, someone else might be injured. You should make sure everyone is okay, and if anyone is hurt, make sure the person gets the help he or she needs.

Staying at the scene and making sure everyone involved is okay is just the right thing to do, but besides that, leaving the scene of an accident is against the law, and you could get arrested for it.

Don't forget to call the police. You may think the accident was minor. You may think nobody was injured. The damage to the cars may not seem like a big deal. It may seem like calling the police to report the accident is overkill. You are wrong.

About 20 percent of Washington drivers have no liability insurance. Even if the driver who hit you produces an insurance card, it may have lapsed or expired. Even if the other driver offers to take care of your damages himself, you should *always* call the police. If the police come to the scene, they can accurately document the accident and all of the people involved, including witnesses. Even if they decline to come to the scene, there will be a record of your call, which will ultimately strengthen your claim.

If you don't call the police from the scene, what proof do you have that it happened? What if the other driver denies the accident altogether? Calling the police begins to establish a record that the accident actually happened. This record will ultimately help your lawyer make a claim on your behalf and, hopefully, get you a recovery for your injuries.

Don't argue about the cause of the accident. Often following a crash, people's tempers are high. You may feel that the other driver was careless, and you may be right. But being aggressive toward the other driver, yelling at him or getting in his face, will not help your cause. In fact, it could hurt you if witnesses testify at trial that you were jumping around or were being aggressive at the scene of the wreck.

Stay calm, assess the situation, and make sure everyone involved is okay. Take photos, exchange information, call the police, and remain safe. Ultimately, who is at fault for causing the accident will get sorted out. Losing your cool will not have any effect on that determination, other than to make you look bad.

Don't tell people it was your fault. The reality is that legal fault for causing a motor vehicle accident can be complicated. Just like you can't know for sure what your injuries are until you are examined by a doctor, you really can't know all of the legal factors involved in determining fault until you consult an experienced personal injury attorney.

Accepting fault for causing the accident is a legal admission of liability and can be used against you later, not only to prevent you from making a recovery, but also to support claims for damages against you. Stay calm and make sure everyone is okay, but don't accept liability for the accident at the scene.

Don't forget to document EVERYTHING. One of the most common mistakes I see is people leaving the scene of the accident without getting all of the documentation they need. In order to advance a claim for damages, the more information you gather and document, the better off you will be. You should document the location of the collision, the vehicles involved, including make, model, color, and license number, the people involved, including drivers, passengers, and witnesses, the damage to the vehicles, and the drivers' licenses and insurance policies involved. You should get the other driver's address and phone number. You should photograph *everything*.

If there were witnesses, especially if they support your version of the events, you *must* document their names and contact information. I can't tell you how many times I've had clients who swear there was a witness, but they failed to take down his or her name and number. You never know how a claim will go, and what might make the difference between getting a fair recovery and getting nothing at all. At the scene is your only opportunity to document the information necessary to move your case smoothly forward.

BUT MY HEADLIGHTS WERE ON

Sometimes a witness can make the difference between having a winning case and not having a case at all. Brian Santorini came to see me for a consultation following a collision in an unrestricted intersection. He swore he was well into the intersection when another car T-boned him. The other driver and his passenger claimed that Brian was driving without headlights and couldn't be seen. Fortunately, there was a witness who helped Brian out of his car after the impact, and who must certainly have seen that Brian's headlights were still on, even after the crash.

The problem was that Brian never got the witness' contact information or even his name. Without that information, it was Brian's word against the other two, and the case went nowhere.

Remember, when you are making a claim for damages, you have the burden of proving who is at fault for the collision. With the adrenaline blast following an accident, and with the possibility of injuries, it's easy to forget to document everything, but failing to do so could make a decent claim evaporate into thin air.

CONCLUSION

Being involved in a motor vehicle collision can be frightening and confusing. Knowing what to do and what not to do in advance can make the aftermath much less distressing. By taking these few simple steps at the scene, you can insure that you are following the law, protecting your rights, and maximizing your chances to make a recovery if you are injured. At the conclusion of this book is a one-page guide of what to do immediately following a car wreck. I encourage you to remove this page and make copies for every vehicle your family owns. Share it with your friends and relatives. It just might make the difference in the event of an unexpected accident.

CHAPTER 5

GETTING THE TREATMENT YOU NEED

EMTs learned to love brave patients—they weren't nearly such a pain in the ass as the whiners—but not to trust them. In the name of courage, they would hide symptoms, not ask for help when there was help hovering around them anxious to give them succor....

— Nevada Barr

In Chapter 4, we focused on the scene of the collision. Without adequate documentation of the injuries, property damage, witnesses, and parties involved, you may not be able to make a full recovery, or even pursue your claim at all. In this chapter, I will discuss the importance of obtaining appropriate medical treatment following your injury. This includes both emergency treatment and an ongoing treatment plan until you are restored to pre-injury status, or as close to it as you can be.

I'VE BEEN THERE

November 21, 2002 was a typical November evening. It was dark and rainy, and traffic on northbound Interstate 5 in Seattle was heavy. I was driving home from work, and I was very aware of the Volvo that had been tailgating me for the last mile or so. Suddenly, the traffic ahead of me came to a stop. I was able to stop my 1998 Mustang, but the driver of the Volvo behind me never even hit his brakes. He smashed into the rear of my car. The impact pushed my Mustang into a large SUV ahead of me. My car's rear-end was crunched in, and the trailer hitch from the SUV split my front bumper in two.

Right away, I knew I was hurt. I felt tightness in my neck and right shoulder, and in my left lower back. I stayed in my car until the medics arrived, and they placed me into a cervical collar and back-board. I was transported by ambulance to the emergency room at Virginia Mason Medical Center, where I was x-rayed and ex-amined. The doctor prescribed some pain medication and muscle relaxants, and he instructed me to follow-up if the pain didn't re-solve. That's pretty typical for an ER.

I followed up with a chiropractor and began a course of chiroprac-tic and massage therapy. At this point, I was pretty sure my prima-ry injury was just a strain to my neck and upper back. Over the next few months, I continued my treatment, but as the pain and stiffness in my neck and upper back improved, the left lower back pain continued to worsen. Shooting pains were radiating into my left hip and down my leg all the way to my toes, and the muscles in my hip and leg were continuously spasming. It was around this time I decided to hire a lawyer to represent me.

My chiropractor sent me for a lumbar spine MRI, which showed disc bulges and protrusions at multiple levels. The most significant was an annular tear of the disc at L5-S1, which resulted in a protru-sion that was coming into contact with the nerve root. This contact was the cause of the pain, which continued to radiate down my leg.

Based on the results of the MRI, I was referred to a physiatrist, a specialist in rehabilitation and physical medicine. That doctor ordered more diagnostic testing and prescribed new medications for the pain. He also ordered a course of physical therapy.

The physical therapy was excruciating, and during that time, I was in unbearable pain. At times, I was unable to roll from my back to my side. I couldn't lift, twist, sit for any extended period, run, or participate in any kinds of sports. I could barely get into and out of my car.

Within a few weeks of starting physical therapy, I got my first epidural steroid injection at the L5-S1 level. This injection helped a lot, and I was able to continue physical therapy. Each time the symptoms returned, I received another injection, ultimately getting seven injections over a period of two and a half years.

During that time, I met with an orthopedic surgeon, who offered to perform surgery on my injured spine, but I did not like the odds he gave me. This doctor told me I had an 80 percent chance of a full recovery, 15 percent chance of no change, and a 5 percent chance of permanent worsening. Because the injections were effectively managing the pain, I was not willing to risk a one in twenty chance that it would be permanently worse. Instead, I continued the injections and physical therapy.

In September, 2003, almost a year after the accident, my insurance company requested that I attend an independent medical examination. My lawyer and I agreed that the risk of attending the examination was minimal. Following the exam, the insurance company doctor documented weakness and atrophy in my left leg. He also documented muscle spasms and diminished range of motion. He noted that the tear to my disc would be a weak or vulnerable spot that would be more susceptible to damage in any future injury. Based on this report, my PIP coverage continued to pay my accident-related bills.

By March, 2004, I had lost over thirty pounds of excess fat and strengthened my core considerably. I continued to experience major flare-ups of pain and disability, but I was increasingly able to enjoy my life, and I gradually resumed most of my pre-accident activities.

In 2004, my lawyer negotiated a policy limits settlement with the insurance company for the Volvo that hit me, and shortly after, I agreed to an additional settlement from my own underinsured motorist coverage (UIM). The money certainly didn't undo the harm I suffered, but it paid the bills, made up for the time I had to spend away from my growing law practice, and allowed me to set something aside for the future.

Since my settlement, I have continued to focus on keeping my weight down and my core strong. I find this is the best way to keep the pain at bay. To this day, my lower back continues to flare up after strenuous activity, but the flare-ups eventually resolve, and I am able to live the life I want to live and be an active father to my young son.

My point is that we rarely know the extent of our injuries—or even whether we are injured—following an accident. If medical treatment is offered at the scene, it should *always* be accepted. It may be inconvenient, and you may have other things to do, but it is important that you at least get checked out. If you are not offered help at the scene, you should get yourself to the emergency room or at least to your primary care physician as quickly as possible.

Seeking medical help is important for three reasons. First, you may have suffered a serious, even life-threatening injury and not be aware of it. If you have a fractured spine, internal bleeding, or other types of injuries that are left untreated, you could end up with serious problems. An initial examination will rule out any such dangerous or life-threatening conditions. Second, an exam will give you peace of mind that you are not more seriously injured. It is far better to take the time and know that you are okay than to assume you are okay initially, and then wonder later. Finally, a medical professional will likely be able to advise you on how you can minimize any discomfort following the accident and how to get back to normal as quickly as possible.

WALKING ON A BROKEN HEEL

Belinda Moore was driving her car through an intersection in Seattle when another car ran a red light and T-boned her. Belinda jammed her foot on the brake, and the impact was so strong, it literally snapped the bone of her heel. Belinda was on her way to work, and although it hurt, she declined an ambulance and continued to her job. She spent that day working from a chair with her foot elevated; when she made it home, she lay down on the couch. She thought about going to the hospital, but she already had a doctor appointment scheduled for a few days later, so she endured the pain and waited for her appointment.

Ultimately, it took a series of x-rays to diagnose the injury properly, and Belinda spent more than a week walking on her broken heel. Once the injury was diagnosed, it took multiple surgeries, and cumulatively more than a year in a cast, completely non-weight bearing, before Belinda's heel was fully healed.

When Belinda sought my help, we quickly exhausted the liability insurance for the driver who hit her, but it was a struggle to get anything from her underinsured motorist coverage. The insurance company argued that it was not the crash, but a pre-existing condition that caused the broken heel. It even hired an orthopedic surgeon to say the injury wasn't from this car accident.

Ultimately, we had to arbitrate the claim before a panel of three arbitrators. We presented all of the evidence, including excellent testimony from Belinda's foot surgeon, and the insurance company had its expert testify that the injury was not related. The arbitrators concluded that the injury was, in fact, caused by the crash, but they were concerned that Belinda did not seek medical treatment immediately after the accident. Although she made a pretty good recovery, I am convinced she would have been awarded more for her pain and suffering had she sought appropriate medical care right away rather than waiting until her previously scheduled appointment.

NO TREATMENT—NO CASE

Sometimes, a potential new client contacts me regarding an injury claim. The person describes the accident and how he was injured, and then he tells me that although he has been hurting for months or even years, he has not received any treatment for his injuries. He often has very good reasons for not getting treatment. Sometimes, he has no insurance and can't afford to see a doctor. Sometimes, he or she is a single parent working a full-time job who didn't have time to go to the doctor.

Everyone has his own particular circumstances, and everyone has to make the choices that are best for himself and his family. But these decisions have consequences. If your accident was a year ago—or even six months ago—and you have not seen a doctor, there's probably not much a lawyer can do for you. When you are making a claim for an injury, you need to prove not only that the accident took place and that it was the other guy's fault, but that you were injured and that your injuries were caused by the accident. This proof comes in the form of medical records and your doctor's opinion. Without medical treatment, you have neither medical records nor a doctor's opinion. Even if you start seeing a doctor long after the accident, there is no way to prove no intervening cause exists for your injuries.

Of course, there are exceptions to every rule. Perhaps a surgeon left an instrument in your abdomen and it was not causing symptoms until recently. Perhaps an auto accident weakened a joint that started causing you pain much later. These situations do arise, and if they can be established with medical evidence, they could still be good cases, but for the most part, if you are hurt and don't get treatment, it will be extremely difficult, if not impossible, for a lawyer to get you a recovery.

It must be noted here that I am not suggesting, nor would I ever suggest, that anyone get medical treatment he doesn't need. Getting unnecessary medical treatment just to build up a claim is fraud, and I won't have anything to do with that. Also, I also do not prescribe treatment. I'm a lawyer, not a doctor. When a client or potential client asks me what kind of treatment he should get, I tell him to go to his doctor so they can create a treatment plan together.

My point is, if you were in an accident, even a minor one, it is imperative that you get checked out by a medical professional. After that, if you are experiencing any pain, stiffness, or physical limitation, you should be getting some kind of medical treatment. If you don't, you're not only prolonging the pain and delaying your recovery, but you are harming your legal claim and reducing your chances of getting a fair recovery.

POST-ACCIDENT TREATMENT CHOICES

You should know a few things about post-accident medical treatment because the care and treatment you get from different types of providers can vary significantly.

The *Emergency Room* is focused on ruling out permanent and life-threatening injuries. If you have a fractured vertebra, a punctured lung, a torn ligament, or a broken foot, it is likely that the ER doctors will diagnose this problem and prescribe a course of treatment that involves medical specialists, advanced diagnostics, and possibly even surgery. However, the ER personnel are not particularly concerned about less severe injuries that may cause you significant pain and disability for months. If you have an injury to your neck or back from the violent forces your body experienced in the accident, it may be ignored or overlooked by the ER personnel. They'll probably prescribe you pain medication and muscle relaxants and advise you to follow-up with a doctor if your symptoms persist or worsen.

That's why you should always get checked out by *your regular physician* after your ER visit. And if you feel your injuries are not serious enough to justify a visit to the hospital, you should *definitely* get checked out by your primary care doctor as soon as possible following the accident. A doctor can prescribe chiropractic, physical therapy, massage, or other treatment that might help you recover more quickly. Your visit to the doctor also demonstrates to the insurance company that you consider your injuries serious enough to seek treatment. This visit will be important later when you are trying to negotiate a settlement to your claim. While no one should get unnecessary treatment, the failure to get necessary care following an injury can significantly reduce the value of your legitimate claim.

As with the ER, a medical doctor can really do only a few things for your injuries. Of course, he or she can help diagnose your condition and recommend further treatment, but for sprains, strains, or other types of whiplash or soft-tissue injuries, the best a physician can do is to prescribe medication and refer you for additional treatment. It is that treatment that, ultimately, may determine how long it takes you to get better and whether you suffer from any residual problems.

Depending on your injuries, you may be referred for diagnostic imaging, to a specialist, such as an orthopedist, physiatrist, or neurologist, or you may be referred to chiropractic, physical therapy, massage, acupuncture, or some other type of treatment. While it is important, both for your physical wellbeing and the success of your legal claim, that you follow your doctor's advice, you should always remember that *you are in charge of your medical care*. Nobody knows your body better than you do. If a doctor tells you there is nothing wrong, but you know there is, seek a second opinion. If a doctor refers you for a type of treatment that makes you uncomfortable, let the doctor know how you feel and discuss alternatives. The worst thing you can do is simply to ignore your doctor's advice.

In my experience with whiplash-type injuries, two different treatment routes can be chosen. Each is valid, and each has its advantages and disadvantages. Ultimately, it will be up to you and your doctors to decide which type of treatment is the best fit for you.

The first route involves *physical therapy* with periodic follow-up visits with your physician. Physical therapy can help to restore muscle function and range of motion, and it can restore strength following an injury. If you do choose physical therapy, it is important to maintain periodic re-evaluations with your physician to make sure the treatment is providing a benefit.

The second route I commonly see is a combination of *chiropractic* and *massage therapy*. In my experience, this combination provides the fastest and most lasting relief from the pain and limitations associated with soft tissue injuries. Unfortunately, the insurance companies generally don't have the same respect for chiropractors as they do for other types of doctors. If you do choose the chiropractic route, make sure you periodically check in with your primary care doctor, and make sure he or she knows you are receiving treatment from a chiropractor. Ratification and endorsement of this treatment by a medical doctor is often the factor that allows you to obtain full compensation for your injuries.

A wide range of less traditional treatment is available to you following an injury. Such treatment includes naturopathy, homeopathy, acupuncture, hypnotherapy, energy work, and much more. I am certainly not an expert on any kind of medical treatment, but I am a strong advocate that injured people know what is best for them, and they are in the best position to make medical decisions. From a legal perspective, you are more likely to make a good recovery for your injuries if all of your treatment is coordinated, or at least ratified, by a medical doctor.

CONCLUSION

In summary, several compelling reasons exist to get prompt medical evaluation and treatment following an accident:

1. To identify any serious or possibly life-threatening injuries

2. To provide peace of mind by ruling out any such serious conditions

3. To map out an appropriate course of treatment early

4. To obtain necessary referrals for diagnostics or medical specialists

5. To demonstrate to the insurance companies that you take your injuries seriously enough to seek medical treatment

You should remember that while you are in charge of your medical treatment, you should never ignore a doctor's advice or fail to show up for scheduled appointments. Doing so could delay or hinder your recovery, and it will certainly affect your ability to get full compensation in your legal claim.

Finally, whatever kind of treatment you decide to receive for your injuries, you should include a medical doctor in your treatment plan, and you should receive periodic re-evaluations from that medical doctor. Your doctor will insure that your treatment stays on track, and the evaluations will strengthen your claim against the insurance company.

On the lines below, make a list of the health care providers you have seen in connection with your accident. This list will help ensure your lawyer gets a complete list of providers when she is preparing your claim.

_____
_____
_____
_____
_____
_____
_____
_____
_____
_____
_____
_____
_____

CHAPTER 6
GETTING YOUR MEDICAL BILLS PAID

My doctor gave me six months to live, but when I couldn't pay the bill he gave me six months more.

— Walter Matthau

In the previous chapter, I discussed the importance of getting the appropriate medical evaluation and treatment following an accident. As I briefly mentioned, one of the biggest reasons people don't get the treatment they need is the very legitimate concern about how their bills will be paid. When people don't have the money to pay their medical bills, and they don't want to go into debt, they often forego necessary medical treatment. Such a decision, while entirely reasonable, can prolong their pain and make it difficult or even impossible for a lawyer to get them fair compensation for their claim. This chapter addresses the various ways injured people can get the medical treatments they need regardless of their financial situations.

When you are injured in an accident, several options exist for getting your bills paid. Of course, the person who caused the accident, or that person's liability insurer, is ultimately responsible for your bills, but he won't pay as you go. Instead, he or his insurance company will make one payment, at the conclusion of your claim, for all of your damages including your medical bills. Until then, you have many options to get your bills paid. The first option is some kind of no-fault coverage such as personal injury protection (PIP) or medical payments coverage (MedPay). This is also usually the best option because with PIP coverage, there are no co-pays, deductibles, or network limitations. That is why, in Chapter 3, I urged you to maximize your PIP coverage. If you were a pedestrian, bicyclist, or passenger, you may be covered by the driver's PIP coverage. Likewise, if you are injured at someone's home or place of business, you may be covered by the property owner's MedPay coverage. A good lawyer will be able to determine very quickly whether such coverages exist.

If there is no PIP or MedPay, or if that coverage is exhausted, the next best option is individual or group health insurance. This insurance is provided by your employer or purchased for your family. Anyone can obtain health insurance for his family, and if you meet certain financial thresholds, you may qualify for free or steeply discounted health insurance from the State. Unfortunately, if you've already been injured before you had health insurance, it may be difficult to get full coverage.

When there is no PIP or MedPay coverage and no health insurance, things start to get more difficult; however, there is always a way to get the treatment you need. One option is to get treatment on a lien. That means you get treatment from a doctor or therapist who agrees to carry a balance, which you agree to pay in full at the conclusion of your case. The benefit of this arrangement is that you can get the treatment you need now, without any out-of-pocket expense. This arrangement will help you recover more quickly from your injuries, and it will make it more likely that you get full monetary compensation on your claim. The downside is that many providers, especially medical specialists, are reluctant to treat on a lien, and if you lose your case, or you fail to make an adequate recovery, you remain responsible for your outstanding balance. While this is certainly a risk that must be considered, in a strong case, the risk is well-justified by the benefits you will get from the treatment. When doctors refuse to provide treatment on a lien, there are a few specialized companies that will pay the doctors now and carry the balance for future payment from your recovery.

Finally, while not advisable, if you absolutely need treatment and can't get it anywhere else, you can always go to the emergency room. Emergency rooms are required to provide medical evaluation and appropriate treatment to everyone who presents with a legitimate medical problem. If you can demonstrate true financial hardship, many hospitals will agree to reduce or completely write off your medical bills.

While many options exist for getting medical treatment following an accident, it can be confusing or even overwhelming trying to figure out what to do while dealing with the pain of your injuries and trying to take care of your family. The best thing to do is consult with an experienced personal injury lawyer as soon as possible after your accident. He will be able to determine what payment options are available, explain the risks and benefits of each, and help you make the decisions that will provide the maximum benefit for you and your family.

THE COWBOY

Justin McCall was self-employed in an extremely physical and demanding field. He was the sole earner in his family, and he had no PIP coverage and no health insurance. While standing in a parking lot, he was struck by a car and thrown thirty feet. He was imme-diately transported to the emergency room, and he followed up his ER visit with chiropractic treatment. After several months of intensive chiropractic treatment with little improvement, he asked me for help.

Justin told me he was basically unable to work because of the pain from his neck and back injuries. He was struggling to pay his bills, and he didn't know what to do. I told him his case was strong. A witness had observed the driver speeding through the parking lot trying to get a spot so there was no doubt who was at fault for caus-ing the accident. However, without appropriate treatment, it would be impossible for me to get fair value for his injuries. He was con-cerned about running up additional debt for medical treatment. This is certainly a legitimate concern, and I could not make any guarantees, but I told him I felt it was very likely we would recover more than enough to cover all of his medical bills.

Ultimately, Justin agreed to get an MRI. We were able to locate a facility that would perform the MRI on a lien, meaning it would hold the balance until the conclusion of his case in exchange for a letter of protection. A letter of protection is basically a letter from the attorney guaranteeing that at the time of settlement, the med-ical bills will be paid in full before any money is disbursed to the patient. Unfortunately, in this case, the MRI confirmed our worst fears. Justin had multiple herniated discs in his neck. These discs were putting pressure on Justin's nerves and causing intense pain.

Based on the findings on his MRI, Justin agreed to get more ag-gressive treatment. We found a specialist who would treat him on a lien, and he underwent a series of epidural steroid injections, coupled with a course of physical therapy. It was a long road to recovery, but ultimately, Justin was able to return to work.

Although it was a close call, Justin was able to avoid bankruptcy, and he did not lose his house. Based on his treatment records, we were able to obtain a recovery that was more than adequate to pay all of the outstanding medical bills and to compensate Justin for his pain and for the emotional anguish that the injury caused for his whole family.

If Justin had not come to me looking for creative options to pay for his necessary medical treatment, he may not have recovered from his injuries. He certainly wouldn't have obtained a fair recovery from the insurance company, even though it was clear that the driver was responsible.

WHY WON'T MY DOCTOR BILL MY INSURANCE?

As I stated above, PIP or MedPay is the best option to pay for accident-related medical treatment. With this kind of coverage, there is no deductible, no copay, no network, and no referral requirement. The only requirement is that the treatment be reasonable, accident-related, and medically necessary. But when there is no PIP or MedPay, or when that coverage is exhausted, health insurance becomes the primary option for paying your bills. While health insurance is not as beneficial as PIP, it does provide significant advantages for you as the patient. Most health insurers have negotiated steep reductions in repayment rates with their participating providers. That means if you get a $100 treatment and pay a $20 copay, the insurance doesn't actually pay the remaining $80. Instead, it pays something like $40 or even less, and the remaining balance gets written off. As you can imagine, doctors don't like this reduction very much, but in exchange for agreeing to these terms, they get the benefit of being listed on the insurance company's website, and getting all of the additional business that generates.

Occasionally, I run into a situation where my client has no PIP coverage, but he does have health insurance. He seeks out a provider in his insurance network and begins treatment, only to be told by the doctor's office: "We don't bill insurance on auto claims." The reason for this is clear. The provider would rather carry the balance and charge you the full amount for each treatment, often with interest added, rather than accept the reduced amount the insurance company will pay. A couple of problems result from this situation. First, our client has paid for the benefit that health insurance provides—namely, reduced out-of-pocket cost. When the doctor refuses to bill our client's health insurance, he is essentially trying to steal from the client. Second, in order to become a participating provider with an insurance company, a doctor signs a contract that requires her to bill health insurance for all covered treatments and procedures. Refusal to bill the insurance is actually a violation of this contract and could result in the doctor being removed from the insurance network.

Sometimes, doctors aggressively refuse to bill insurance, threatening to withhold or terminate treatment unless the patient and his or her lawyer agree in writing that the doctor's bills will be paid in full, regardless of insurance coverage. In situations like this, I advise my clients to seek out other doctors who will honor their contracts, but when the charges have already been incurred, I work aggressively to make sure my clients get the full benefit they have paid for in the form of health insurance premiums. First, I reach out to the doctors and remind them of their legal and contractual obligation to bill the insurance. I point out to them that if they delay for too long in submitting their bills to the insurance company and the charges are denied for being submitted too late, my client does not have to pay anything. If the doctor continues to refuse, I contact the insurance company to confirm that the doctor is, in fact, a participating provider and that she is required to bill insurance. If I get confirmation from the insurance company, I ask it to follow up with the doctor. This follow-up almost always resolves the situation.

If you have health insurance and your doctor is refusing to bill your insurance following an accident, contact a lawyer right away and consider finding a new doctor. You've paid for that insurance, so you deserve to get the benefits you paid for. I'm the first to admit this situation isn't ideal for the doctor, but as long as she is signing contracts with insurance companies, she is required to honor the terms of those contracts, even when your injuries are the result of an accident.

CONCLUSION

Too often, I see clients who have gone months without getting the medical treatment they need because they are afraid of the financial hardship those medical bills might create. If you were injured in an accident, there are almost always ways you can get the treatment you need. If you're not sure what to do, call a personal injury lawyer for help. If there is insurance that can be used to pay your bills, your lawyer will make sure the insurance company does so. Experienced lawyers know how the insurance companies look at injury claims, and it is often differently than you'd expect. In the next chapter, we will discuss looking at your claim the way your insurance company does.

CHAPTER 7
LOOKING AT YOUR CASE LIKE AN INSURANCE COMPANY

Insurance: An ingenious modern game of chance in which the player is permitted to enjoy the comfortable conviction that he is beating the man who keeps the table.

— Ambrose Bierce

You may think you have an automatic, sure thing, slam dunk claim. The facts are so clear, your injuries are so obvious, and your treatment was so reasonable that nobody could possibly take issue with any part of your claim. After twenty years practicing personal injury law, I can tell you there is no such thing as a sure thing. Even with obvious liability, serious injuries, and reasonable medical treatment, I have seen insurance companies offer less than the medical bills or even refuse to make an offer at all. While you are looking at your case in a vacuum, thinking only about how your life has been affected, the insurance company is looking at the big picture, and your claim is one of thousands just like it around the country.

THE CANOE TRIP

In Chapter 1, I mentioned the wilderness camp I attended during my early teenage years. At this camp, we'd spend the weekends resting and preparing for our next adventure; then on Monday, we'd head out into the wilderness for another week-long trip. One of my favorite trips was canoeing on the Delaware River. We'd start at Barryville, on the New York-Pennsylvania state line, and paddle our way down the river to Port Jervis, a twenty-mile stretch with mostly Class 1 and some Class 2 rapids.

We'd spend Sunday at camp preparing our food for the week, packing our clothes and gear, and doing our best to make sure everything was water-tight. Surely, if we did that, we'd be fine and have a great time. We didn't realize at the time that our counselors were thinking about where we'd camp each night, what we would do if someone's gear got wet or lost, how we might handle an emergency illness or injury, and a hundred other questions that never occurred to us as campers.

From the campers' point of view, it was simple. Pack your gear and go. But from the counselors' point of view, it was a whole different set of problems. I'm fairly certain the park rangers and game wardens who patrolled the river also viewed our trip in an entirely different light.

Likewise, you and I may view your injury claim as simple and straightforward. You were hit. It was someone else's fault. You were injured, and you deserve compensation. The insurance company, always looking to maximize profit, views your case as one of many, and regardless of the particular facts of your claim, it is looking to drive behavior that will reduce claims in the long run.

So what is the insurance company and its representatives thinking?

PROFIT, PROFIT, PROFIT

The first thing to realize is that insurance companies, like most corporations, are motivated by one thing: the desire to maximize profit. This desire is not necessarily good or bad; it's just a fact. The insurance company doesn't care about you or how your life was affected by your injuries. If it can get away with paying you less than you deserve—or nothing at all—it will.

This profit motive can work to your advantage as well. Insurance companies are required to negotiate in good faith. If they refuse to do so, they could be on the hook for thousands of dollars in additional damages. Further, it costs a lot to take a case to trial. Even where the big insurance companies have lawyers on staff, collecting a fixed salary, going to trial involves hiring expert witnesses, preparing exhibits, and investing significant time that could be used resolving other claims. If your lawyer can persuade the insurance company that the risks and expenses of litigation outweigh the cost of making a reasonable settlement, the insurance company will relent. Often the persuasion process can take months, or even years, but ultimately, insurance companies will make the decisions that are financially best for them.

There's another factor working here as well.

You look at your claim in a vacuum. You were hurt. It was someone else's fault. You got treatment. You missed work. You couldn't do the things you wanted to do. You deserve to be compensated for your loss. Simple, right?

Well, as we discussed above, the insurance company looks at your claim in the context of thousands of other claims around the country. Perhaps it believes that by creating delays and expenses in certain types of claims, it will discourage other attorneys from taking those claims. Perhaps it believes that by making it extremely difficult to get a fair settlement, people will "take what they can get" and abandon their claims.

Ultimately, it's impossible to know just what the insurance company is thinking. In reality, a corporation doesn't "think" at all. It has policies, procedures, and guidelines all designed to maximize the bottom line and satisfy the shareholders. Sometimes in the context of a particular case, those policies make no sense at all, but you can be sure the insurance companies will do what they think is best for them, not for you.

COMMISSIONED SALESMEN

In the sales industry, workers make more money when they sell more stuff, bringing more money into the company. In the claims business, adjusters are motivated by keeping more money in the company. Claims adjusters are evaluated, promoted, and rewarded for paying out as little as possible on claims. In fact, those who pay out the least are often rewarded with bonuses, vacations, and even promotions to supervisory positions.

Different adjusters use different tactics to accomplish this goal. Some are sweet and cooperative on the phone, reassuring you that everything will be taken care of if you just work with them. These adjusters are hoping you'll trust that they are on your side and that you will not consult with an attorney. When and if they do make you an offer, you can be sure it won't be for the full value of your claim.

Other adjusters are nasty and confrontational, making you feel like the person at fault and questioning everything you do. These adjusters may criticize your choices of medical treatment and try to scare you into cutting your treatment short because it might "hurt your claim." They may dismiss the impact your injuries have had on your life, and they may encourage you to settle right away.

Finally, other adjusters just ignore you. They are impossible to reach. You always reach their voicemail boxes, and they never return your calls. When you do finally reach them, you often discover that your claim has been reassigned to a different adjuster who doesn't know anything about you or your situation.

The tactics may be different, but the goal is the same: to make you and your claim go away for as little money as possible.

Never trust an insurance claims adjuster. Always assume his or her motivations are different from yours. If you have a claim, no matter how obvious you think it might be, consult an experienced attorney. When people contact my office after they've been speaking with the insurance company, I tell them whether they're being treated fairly. (It does happen occasionally.) If I don't think I can improve their position and make the process easier for them, I tell them so. But almost every time, I can free them from the hassle and uncertainty of trying to handle their claims on their own, and I can put more money in their pockets than they would get if they try to deal with the insurance companies on their own.

"BUT WHAT IF IT'S *MY* INSURANCE COMPANY?"

In an earlier chapter, I discussed uninsured/underinsured motorist coverage and personal injury protection coverage. These are "first-party" coverages, meaning they are part of your policy with your own insurance company.

Clients come to me all the time saying things like "I've been paying my monthly premium to this company for twenty-five years. I've been a loyal customer, and I'm sure it will treat me fairly."

Think again.

Your insurance company wants you to think it is your best friend. It will tell you you're in good hands or that it is a good neighbor. It might even treat you well when you have a minor claim for a chipped windshield or a damaged mirror. But don't have any doubt; once you ask the insurance company—any insurance company—for money, it becomes your adversary.

With PIP coverage, where your insurance company is paying for your accident-related medical bills, it will take any opportunity to argue that your treatment is not reasonable, not accident-related, or both. It will take a recorded statement from you and use your words against you. It will require you to be examined by its doctors, who are chosen because they frequently say what the insurance company wants to hear: that your treatment is not reasonable or accident-related, and that the insurance company should not pay for it.

Likewise, with uninsured or underinsured motorist coverage, your insurance company is acting as the insurer for the uninsured driver who caused your injuries. As such, it will make any argument and use any tactic to diminish your recovery, or to deny you any recovery at all. This is an adversarial system, and when you make a claim against an insurance company—even your own—its objective is to defeat your claim.

You may be loyal to your insurance company, but be assured that your insurance company is not loyal to you.

THE INSURANCE COMPANY IS THREATENING TO CLOSE MY CLAIM

The one thing insurance companies don't want is for you to be educated about your rights. An educated claimant knows what he has to say and what he can keep private. He knows what forms he has to sign and what forms can be discarded. An educated claimant cannot be bullied by the insurance companies, but someone who doesn't know his rights can be intimidated into acting too quickly or settling for too little.

Mike Johanssen came to see me some time ago looking for help with his auto claim. He had hoped to negotiate a settlement directly with the insurance company and save some money on the attorney fee. The accident was clearly the other driver's fault, and Mike was clearly hurt. In fact, he was still hurt when he came to see me, and he was actively receiving treatment.

Mike told me the insurance company had made him a "one-time of-fer." It told him that if he didn't accept its offer, it was going to "close the claim." He didn't want the claim to be closed, but he was nowhere near finished with his treatment, and he knew that what was being offered was too low. I explained to Mike that "closing the claim" really didn't mean anything. In Washington, a claimant has three years from the date of the incident to file a lawsuit, and the insurance company can "re-open" the claim at any time.

Regardless, Mike was convinced that the insurance company would neither be honest with him about his rights, nor negotiate his claim in good faith without a lawyer backing him up. He retained my services, and I immediately notified the insurance company that I was representing him. To date, the claim remains open, and when Mike is finished with his treatment and he and I know the full extent of his injuries and how they impacted his life, we will explore a negotiated settlement with the insurance company. If we can't settle, we'll take them to court. It is that threat that will keep the insurance company honest throughout the process and insure that Mike's rights are protected.

CONCLUSION

Your case may appear simple to you and me, but insurance companies have a different agenda, and they view your claim differently. To move your claim forward in the most effective manner, you must understand how the insurance company sees your claim, and what factors are motivating its decisions. With this knowledge, you and your attorney can present your claim in a way that will properly motivate the insurance company to deal fairly with you and make you a reasonable offer of settlement. Without this information, you could be intimidated or manipulated into sacrificing your rights and compromising the fair value of your injury claim.

CHAPTER 8

DECIDING WHETHER YOU NEED A LAWYER

They say a man who represents himself has a fool for a client.
Well, with God as my witness, I am that fool!

— Gomez Addams, *The Addams Family*

In the previous chapter, I discussed how insurance companies view your case and how that view can differ from your own. In this chapter, I will discuss how to determine whether you need a lawyer to deal with the insurance company on your behalf.

CAMPING WITH BEARS

A few years ago, before our son was born, my wife and I took an extended trip to Alaska. We visited my friend in Anchorage, did some salmon fishing, and camped out in Denali National Park. The highlight of the trip was a stay at remote Brooks Camp in Katmai National Park.

To get to Brooks Camp, we had to take a small plane from Anchorage, and then an even smaller plane to a lake deep in the wilderness. Brooks Camp is set between two lakes connected by a short river with a six-foot-high waterfall halfway between the lakes. If you get there during the salmon run, you can see thousands of salmon jumping the waterfall. You know who else can see the salmon jumping? Grizzly bears. Hundreds of them. The bears congregate around the waterfall to fish for salmon. Some stand above the falls, grabbing the fish after they've successfully made the jump. Some wait a bit downstream and grab the salmon who have failed to make the jump and fallen back into the river. My favorites are the ones who stand right at the falls and grab the salmon from mid-flight as they are jumping.

The camp itself is rustic, but pretty well-established. Small cabins are available, but we camped in a tent. The tent sites are located in an enclosure surrounded by electrified wire, so we felt relatively safe. Other than the wire, no barriers exist between the bears and the human tourists. Of course, the park limits the number of people who can be there at any given time, but it is definitely bear country, and as the rangers told us, the bears always have the right of way.

You might think you could hang out there without any rangers or other expert help if you just use common sense: don't get in the way of the bears, and make sure your food is packed away in airtight containers far from where you sleep. Just be careful and you'll be safe, right? But what you don't know is where the bears might sneak up on you, what kinds of behaviors indicate the bears are agitated and might become aggressive, how to respond when a bear suddenly appears in your path, and what to do in a thousand other situations you can't even anticipate.

One night, my wife was in the river fly-fishing with a ranger. (It was summer in Alaska, and the sun was still up.) Without her noticing, a bear cub wandered next to her. Suddenly, she found herself between a cub and its mother—a very dangerous place to be. Fortunately, the ranger with her knew just what to do. He stood tall and waved his arms around, making himself very big, and he slapped his fishing rod on the surface of the river, yelling "SCAT!" The cub got scared and ran away, and the mother bear followed. If the ranger hadn't been there, who knows what might have happened to my wife.

Your injury claim is very much like Brooks Camp. Everything looks orderly and fairly well-established, so it seems like if you just use common sense, you can get through it just fine. You might think that any reasonably intelligent person could protect his family, work at his job, go to his medical appointments, and deal with the insurance company, ultimately negotiating a good settlement. Sometimes, it might even work out that way. But do you know what issues the claims adjuster might use to undermine your claim? Do you know when you have to provide information and when you don't? Can you anticipate when the claims adjuster is about to pounce and blow your claim apart? Have you considered the hours you might have to spend researching, documenting, and arguing with the insurance company instead of spending that time with your family, or simply healing and getting better? Just like at Brooks Camp, too many things could go wrong, and the stakes are too high. Having an expert on your side frees you to get better and focus your attention on yourself and your family while giving you the peace of mind that all of the likely pitfalls have been anticipated and your rights are being protected. Hiring an attorney does not guarantee a good outcome, but it makes it much more likely that you won't find yourself in an impossible situation.

A FOOL FOR A CLIENT

Every now and then, someone asks me what was the most import-ant thing I learned in my three years of law school at the University of Washington. My answer, without hesitation, has been the same since I graduated in 1995: "If you have a legal situation, hire an appropriately qualified lawyer."

I know, I know. That advice is biased, and somewhat self-interest-ed. Still, it's the best advice I can give, and it's advice I took myself when I had a personal injury claim, as I stated earlier. When I meet with an accident victim for the first time, I often tell her it's okay if she chooses not to hire me, but it's imperative that she find a lawyer she feels comfortable with to represent her in her claim. The rea-sons are plentiful. The law is complex and an unrepresented per-son could miss something important or give away information she is not legally required to provide. Even more importantly, a skilled attorney will help an injured person evaluate her claim and the in-surance company's position in a more rational, less emotional way than is possible for an injured person (or even a family member) to do on her own.

If you've ever bought or sold a house, you may have thought to yourself, "I can do this. Why should I pay a realtor 3 or 6 percent to do it for me?" The answer is obvious. The transaction is simply too important, and there are too many things that could go wrong to justify doing it yourself. That's not to say people can't successfully buy or sell a house without a realtor—it happens all the time. But for the typical person, the hassle of learning everything you need to know, and the stress of wondering whether you made every re-quired disclosure and completed every required form justifies the expense of hiring a professional.

Likewise, a person certainly could effectively represent herself in an injury claim. It happens all the time. But there is so much to learn, so many rules that must be followed, and so many rights that insurance companies are more than willing to violate if you let them, that the expense of hiring an attorney is almost always justified. A skilled lawyer not only maximizes your recovery, but he relieves you from the burden and the stress of trying to deal with the insurance company on your own. You already have a job and a family. Why try to learn another whole job when an attorney can do it for you?

In my years as an attorney, I've had a few situations where I or a loved one had an injury claim, including claims for major back injuries to myself and my wife resulting from auto accidents. I even tried representing myself and my wife for a short time, but I quickly realized that was a mistake. Although I certainly know how to handle a personal injury claim, when decisions are clouded by anger and indignation, it is impossible to be objective—even for an experienced attorney. Once I hired my own attorney, I was free to focus on recovering from my injuries and being a supportive husband. I have more than once told my wife it's impossible for me to be her loving and supportive husband and her effective attorney at the same time. When it comes to my family, I prefer to be loving and supportive and let someone else do the legal analysis and negotiations or even try the case if necessary.

That's not to say there is no place for anger or indignation, or a deep sense of loss for the effects of an injury in a meaningful analysis of every claim. Indeed, it is an awareness and understanding of the profound loss suffered by the injured person and his family that makes good lawyering possible. However, a good lawyer can objectively provide the injured person and his family with all of the available options and make recommendations based on probabilities and hard experience. This objectivity gives the family members a meaningful counterbalance to their justifiable emotions re-garding their claim, and hopefully, it empowers them to make the decisions that are truly best for them and most effectively facilitate healing and closure from the loss they have suffered.

JUDGE MATT

I am not a judge. I don't want to be a judge, but occasionally, I am called upon to decide a case. In Washington, we have a program of mandatory arbitration for cases valued at less than $50,000. I, like many attorneys, have placed my name on a list of people available to serve as arbitrators in these cases. An arbitration hearing is kind of like a less formal mini-trial. At arbitration, each side is permit-ted to present evidence and call witnesses. At the conclusion of the evidence, each attorney makes a closing argument, connecting all the facts to the applicable law, and tries to persuade the arbitrator to rule in favor of his client.

Over the years, I have served many times as an arbitrator. While I believe everyone who has been injured as a result of someone else's negligence deserves some financial compensation, I approach these hearings with great seriousness, and I require each party ad-equately to prove its case. Usually, the lawyers present their clients' claims with great skill and professionalism, so my decision is based solely on the facts presented.

One time, however, a *pro se* litigant, someone who was representing himself without the assistance of an attorney, made it all the way to an arbitration I was hearing. The claimant was certainly smart, but he was also not a lawyer. His documents were incomplete, his facts were presented in a very disorganized way, and he failed to ask some key questions in examining the witnesses. Ultimately, I took it upon myself to review all of the evidence presented, orga-nize it on my own, and make my best determination. Based on that evidence, I had to rule against the *pro se* claimant. Now, it may be that he would have lost even with an excellent attorney, but I know an attorney would have done a better job trying to persuade me to overlook the key gaps in evidence.

CONCLUSION

Sometimes, it can be appropriate to try representing yourself without the help of a lawyer. Particularly in smaller claims, negotiating a settlement with the insurance company yourself may actually result in a larger net recovery to you. But you need to understand that without a credible threat of a lawsuit, the insurance companies will not make their best offers of settlement. And believe me, an unrepresented person does not pose a credible threat of a lawsuit. If you do try to negotiate a settlement and find you are unable to do so, please don't try to file a lawsuit on your own. Even if you know what you are doing, as I did, you and your family will be better off having a skilled advocate on your side who is less personally affected by the injuries. But even after you've decided to hire a lawyer, your work is not done. Choosing the right lawyer can be a major factor in both your satisfaction with the process and the outcome of your case. In the next chapter, we will discuss how to find the lawyer who is the right fit for you and your family.

CHAPTER 9

FINDING THE RIGHT LAWYER FOR YOU

A lawyer shall act with reasonable diligence
and promptness in representing a client.

— Washington State Rule of Professional Conduct 1.3

In the previous chapter, I discussed whether or not to hire a lawyer. If you've taken my advice and decided to hire a lawyer, you still face an important decision: how do you choose the right lawyer for you? Most people have never needed a lawyer, so they have no personal experience in choosing one. Do you just do a Google search and pick the first name that comes up? Do you look for a useful website with meaningful information? Testimonials? Reviews? Do you ask all of your friends until you find someone with a lawyer to recommend?

I WANT TO FIRE MY LAWYER

Several times each year, I get a call from someone who was injured in an accident, hired a lawyer, and now wants to fire his lawyer and hire me. The most common reason people give for wanting to change lawyers is lack of communication. They tell me stories of trying for weeks to speak to their lawyers without success. They leave messages and speak to case managers, legal assistants, and paralegals. They even send letters, but they never hear back from their attorneys.

This is really a shame because the lawyer being fired might be an excellent advocate, but without good communication, the attorney-client relationship can suffer irreparable harm. I understand why, sometimes, there are lapses in communication between lawyers and their clients. Let's face it; attorneys are busy, and when we get a message to call a client back, it's easy to shuffle that to the bottom of our to-do list and focus our attention on deadlines and other pressing matters. After a while, the message gets lost or it's too late to call back. I don't believe such lapses in communication are ever acceptable. I expect better from my service providers and my clients deserve better from me. In my office, we've instituted a twenty-four-hour call back policy. We no longer give the attorneys messages to return a client's call. Instead, when a client calls to speak to the attorney, he is immediately given a time slot on his lawyer's calendar within the next twenty-four business hours. When the call is on the lawyer's calendar, it can't be ignored or deferred, and when I or any lawyer in my firm is speaking to a client, that client gets 100 percent of our attention.

While lack of communication is the most common reason clients give for wanting to change lawyers, other reasons include loss of confidence, personality conflict, pressure to act against the client's wishes, and more. Most of these problems could have been avoided if the client had been more careful in selecting a lawyer in the first place. Unfortunately, once the lawyer is hired, consequences result from changing your representation.

When I get a call from someone who wants to fire his lawyer and hire me, I try to find out the reason for his dissatisfaction. I explain to him that changing lawyers in the middle of the process can harm his claim in a number of ways. First, the insurance company notes that the lawyer changed, and it tries to use that to undermine the claim. Second, even if you fire your first attorney, you may owe her an attorney fee, depending on the language of your fee agreement. If you have to pay your original attorney and your replacement attorney at the conclusion of your claim, that generally results in less money for you.

In situations like this, I urge the injured person to try to work things out with his original lawyer. Often a face-to-face meeting is all it takes to get things back on track and assure the client that his interests are being protected. Sometimes, however, the damage to the relationship is too severe, or the attorney is simply unresponsive to the client's requests. In those cases, I will agree to take over the representation if the case is strong, and I try to mitigate the harm resulting from having multiple attorneys on the case.

MAKING SURE IT'S A GOOD FIT

The attorney-client relationship can be an intensely personal one, and it can continue for years. You may need to tell your lawyer some unpleasant or secret things about yourself, and you may need to hear difficult truths from him during the course of your case. There is simply no substitute for a face-to-face meeting to help you find the right lawyer for you. I suggest that you meet with several attorneys before making a final decision. It always amazes me that people research and shop for months before buying a new TV or dishwasher, but they hire the first lawyer they meet.

Meet with several lawyers to see who feels like a good fit. Do they listen to you and understand what you hope to accomplish? Do they understand what you and your family are going through? Can they explain in detail how the process will go, and can they answer all of your questions?

When I was in law school, I used to think it was the personal injury lawyer's job to get the most money possible in every single case. Now, having worked with thousands of clients over twenty years, I know that different clients have different needs. Some do want to maximize their financial recovery, and a good lawyer can help them do that. Others want to get the process done quickly and without any further disruption of their lives. Some want a dangerous condition remedied or a dangerous practice stopped. Still others want an apology—often the most difficult outcome to achieve.

The point is that a good lawyer will listen to you and get to know you as a person. Remember, when you hire a lawyer, he is working for you—not the other way around. If he doesn't respect your needs and your goals, you need to find a different lawyer.

Here are a few questions you might want to ask any lawyer you are considering to have represent you in an injury claim:

1.   After I hire you, what do you expect me to do?

It is important that you understand what the lawyer will do for you and what you will need to do for yourself. I tell my clients that their job is to recover from their injuries and get their lives back to normal, and my job is everything else. That means if you get a bill or a collection notice in the mail, you get it to me so I can deal with it. If an insurance company or its representative calls you, you refer him to me. If you have a concern, you let me know. If I don't know about it, I can't do anything about it.

I am also very clear about advising my clients to limit their posts on social media sites while their claim is pending. (More about that later.)

When your treatment is finished, find out whether you are expected to obtain copies of your medical records and other documentation or whether the lawyer will do that for you.

2. After I hire you, what will happen?

Just as important as knowing what you are expected to do is having a clear understanding of what the lawyer will do. A good attorney will be able to explain clearly what will happen in each phase of the representation.

I explain to my clients that while they are still in treatment for their injuries, it is my job to make sure the bills are being paid promptly and by the right insurance company, to protect the client from unwanted contact by the insurance company, and to make sure everything in general is going smoothly.

At the conclusion of the client's medical treatment (which is always a decision made by the client and his or her doctors), I obtain all of the relevant medical records and bills, along with all other necessary documentation.

Once the records are obtained, I prepare a detailed, comprehensive demand package for the insurance company. This package explains why the loss is the company's insured's fault, and explains exactly how my client's life has been affected by the injuries. This package serves two purposes: it gives the insurance company the information it needs to make a fair evaluation of the claim, and it demonstrates that I take the claim seriously and am willing and able to take whatever steps are necessary to get my client a full recovery for his or her loss.

Once my client reviews and approves the demand, I send it to the insurance company with a firm deadline for its response. At that point, the insurance company either makes an opening offer and I engage in negotiations, or it does not make an offer and I file a lawsuit. I will discuss the litigation process later in this book, but my point is that a good lawyer should be able to explain to you what will happen in every phase of your claim and to address every possible situation that might arise. If he can't do that to your satisfaction, you might want to find a different lawyer. At the conclusion of this book is an infographic I call "The Dubin Difference." This document provides an easy-to-follow illustration of each phase of your case and what you should expect.

3. What if I need to speak with you during my claim?

As discussed above, the complaint I hear most often from clients about their attorneys is that they're hard to reach and they don't return calls. It's a simple truth: attorneys can be difficult to reach. We are often in court or meeting with a client, and we can't stop to take every call that comes in, but failing to return calls is inexcusable.

Many law firms utilize case managers, who act as your primary contact during your claim. There certainly is nothing wrong with using a case manager, but what if you really need to speak with your lawyer? What procedures are in place to make sure you get through when you need to?

You deserve to hear from someone in your lawyer's office at least once every month. Even if it's just to see how you're doing and to let you know that nothing has changed, it's important to check in on a regular basis. You also have a right to speak to your lawyer anytime you need to. She may not be able to take your call immediately, but you should get a return call within twenty-four hours. And you should get the lawyer's full attention during the call.

Will you get regular updates from the lawyer you are thinking of hiring? Will she guarantee that you will be able to speak directly with her anytime you need to? If not, maybe you should find a different lawyer.

4.   What kind of medical treatment should I get?

Okay, this is kind of a trick question, but you should ask it anyway. Lawyers are not doctors. We do not prescribe treatment and we do not diagnose injuries. I know there are several ways to treat different types of injuries, and I can certainly make suggestions if requested, but what I generally tell my clients is that they should see a doctor and follow that doctor's advice. If the recommended treatment isn't working after a while, I may recommend they seek out a second opinion.

I can tell my clients what the legal consequences might be of getting $20,000 of acupuncture with no other treatment, or of taking months off from treatment before resuming again, but I never prescribe treatment.

Some attorneys have very close relationships with a particular doctor and insist (or strongly suggest) that you see "their" doctor. In this situation, it's fair for you to ask yourself whose interests the lawyer will be looking out for—yours or the doctor's.

If the person you are meeting with insists that you see a particular doctor or health care provider, perhaps you should consider a different lawyer.

5.   What is this gonna cost me?

Again, this is a question that should be easy to answer, but you may need to do a bit of digging. Almost all lawyers will tell you there is no fee unless they get a recovery for you, but do they mention the costs advanced? Costs advanced are case-related expenses that the attorney advances to move your claim forward. An attorney should be able to explain generally what those costs will be and how you will pay for them.

Also, most attorney fee agreements set forth one fee for settlements (generally one-third) and a higher fee for litigation (generally 40 percent). Your prospective attorney should be able to explain exactly how and when the fee increases, and what that means to you and your net recovery.

I would be especially wary of any attorney who promises you a specific dollar amount in recovery. The simple truth is that we can't guarantee any result, and we can't possibly know the value of your case until your treatment is completed and we know what long term residual effects from your injuries (if any) will remain. If an attorney promises you a specific dollar amount, I'd walk out of that lawyer's office immediately.

THE CLIENT BILL OF RIGHTS

Lawyers will tell you that it is impossible to offer a guarantee in the legal business. WRONG! I believe that all law firm clients should settle for nothing less! Remember, your attorney works for you— not the other way around.

At the Law Offices of Matthew D. Dubin, we confidently promise our clients quality service with personal attention. We believe that as our client, you are entitled to have the following rights. We call it the Client Bill of Rights:

1. The right to loyalty to you and your cause. We are on your side and we are committed to place your interests first— even ahead of our own.

2. The right to be updated regularly and in a timely manner as to the progress of your case. We are committed to having at least one contact with every client every month. At times, it may be necessary to communicate more frequently, but this is a minimum.

3. The right to our respect. We treat every client the way we would want to be treated.

4. The right to expect a high level of competence from our firm and everyone who works here.

5. The right to know the truth about your case. While we are on your side, we will not sugarcoat the truth. We will tell you the good and the bad about your case and empower you to make the best decisions for you and for your family.

6. The right to prompt attention from us. We are absolutely committed to being responsive to our clients' needs. If you call for your attorney and he is not available, we will place you on the calendar for a telephone conference or in-person meeting with your lawyer. This time is set aside just for you.

7. The right to have your legal rights and options explained in plain English without legal mumbo jumbo. It is our job to know the law and to explain it in real-world language to help you understand all of your options.

8. The right to a fair, written fee agreement with our firm. We review every word of our fee agreement with you at the beginning of our relationship. If you have any questions or concerns about our fee agreement at that time, or at any time, we want to know about it.

9. The right to have a fair attorney fee for the work we do. We are proud of the work we perform for our clients, and we believe it has great value, but you have a right to pay a fair fee for your attorney's work. We discuss our fee at the beginning of our relationship, and we believe it represents fair value for the service we provide.

10. The right to make the ultimate decisions on your case. The way we see it, it's our job to provide you with access to the legal system and information that will empower you to make the right decisions for you. We will *never* accept or reject an offer, or make any other major decision regarding the course of your case, without your approval. It is your body that was hurt, and it is your money for which we are fighting. We never forget that we are working for you and not the other way around.

All attorneys in Washington are governed by a code called the Rules of Professional Conduct (RPC). We believe, as attorneys, that we must live by these ethics in all that we do and say.

Among these ethics is one specific right you should be aware of that your lawyer is absolutely required to provide:

Client Confidentiality. This is called the attorney-client privilege. It means that your lawyer, or any member of his or her staff, cannot disclose most things you say or show to your lawyer. This is true if you have hired that lawyer or even if you just talked with a lawyer and communicated certain information. There are exceptions, such as when a person reveals an intent to violate the law in the future, but for the most part, this rule is inviolate.

CONCLUSION

We at the Law Offices of Matthew D. Dubin are committed to the highest standard in legal representation. When you are considering hiring a lawyer, you should ask yourself whether that lawyer will respect you and your rights. Will he be loyal to you and your cause? Will he maintain regular communication with you? Will he explain everything relevant to your case as many times as necessary until you fully understand your rights and your options? Will he explain his fee and insure that it is fair? Will he empower you to make the important decisions regarding your case? If you have concerns about any of these items, perhaps you should keep meeting with attorneys until you find one you are comfortable with. Choosing the right attorney at the beginning of your case can make things much easier down the road. And having peace of mind that your interests are being protected will free you to get better and take care of your family.

CHAPTER 10

OWNING THE CASE

Being in control of your life and having realistic expectations about your day-to-day challenges are the keys to stress management, which is perhaps the most important ingredient to living a happy, healthy and rewarding life.

— Marilu Henner

In the last chapter, we discussed how to select the right lawyer. Choosing a lawyer who is a good fit for you is one of the most important decisions you will make, but regardless of whom you hire, the claim still belongs to you. You have the right to make all of the important decisions regarding your case. In this chapter, I will address your right to make decisions for yourself and your case, even if your attorney disagrees. We will also discuss the responsibility that comes with this decision-making, including the consequences of making poor decisions.

"I WANT TO BREAK YOUR HAND"

When I was in law school, I played in a softball league. The games were pretty casual. It was slow-pitch, and we played mostly for fun. I was the first baseman for my team. During one game, an opposing batter hit a line drive over my head. I jumped up to catch the ball, and when I came down, my mitt slammed down onto the ground. I'm left-handed so the mitt was on my right hand. The hand hurt a little, but I didn't really think much of it. The next inning, I came up to bat. The pitch came in, and the second the aluminum bat struck the ball, I dropped to the ground in agony. It turns out that the impact with the ground had broken a bone in my hand, and the vibration from the bat hitting the ball made it worse.

I went to the emergency room, where I was diagnosed with a broken hand. Eventually, my hand was placed in a cast. After several weeks in the cast, the hand surgeon sat me down to explain why the hand broke. He told me I had a small fatty cyst in the bone of my right hand which weakened the bone and made it susceptible to injury. In order to prevent future fractures, his recommendation was to re-break the bone, remove the fatty cyst, and replace it with bone chips, which would ultimately fuse to the bone and strengthen it. He was sure this was the best thing to do, and he told me that without doing this procedure, I would likely break the bone again in the future.

I knew he was an expert in his field, and I knew very little about broken bones and fatty cysts. It would have been easy just to go along with his advice, but it didn't feel right to me. I had just spent six weeks in a cast, and now he wanted to re-break my hand and put it back in a cast for at least another six weeks. He wanted to do all this to prevent the possibility of a future injury. I asked him how long the cyst had been there, and while he couldn't give me an exact time frame, he said it had probably been there for a long time. I realized that in all that time, I had never broken my hand, and I might never break it again, even without letting him break my hand again.

I did not make a decision immediately. Instead, I considered the doctor's advice, discussed it with my family, and ultimately decided that I'd rather face the risk of a future injury than undergo surgery on my hand and endure another several weeks in a cast. My decision could have been the wrong one. I could have broken my hand again right away and it could have been much worse than the first break. I was responsible for this decision, and I would be responsible for the consequences.

In the twenty years since that incident, do you want to know how many times I've broken my hand? Zero. I continued to play softball and tennis. I camp and hike regularly, and I've taken up golf in the last few years. I've never broken my hand, and I've never even felt soreness at the spot where the doctor said I'd be weak. For me, choosing not to have the surgery was the right decision. Even though the expert told me it was the best thing to do, I took charge of my medical treatment and did what I thought was best. In making that decision, I considered the doctor's advice, and I knew I could be wrong.

When you have an attorney representing you in your personal injury claim, he may make suggestions you disagree with. Your lawyer may be pushing you to file a lawsuit when you really want to settle. Your lawyer may be encouraging you to return to work when you really don't feel ready to go back. Your lawyer may want to handle everything without input from you, but you have a right to know what is happening at all times in your case, and you have a right to give your input to all of the lawyer's decisions.

GOING OVERBOARD

You have a right to know what is happening in your case. It is the lawyer's responsibility to keep you informed and advised of all the developments in your case, whether it's a report from a doctor, a disclosure of policy limits by the insurance company, or a decision to file a lawsuit in a particular court. However, if the lawyer doesn't keep you apprised of what is happening, you can always call to see what's happening. We tell our clients they can call or email any time to ask questions, get a status update, or just to discuss their cases.

Usually, this arrangement works out just fine. We are very conscientious about staying connected with our clients, and when they do call, it's usually to discuss a specific event, such as starting treatment with a new doctor or a change of address. Occasionally, however, things can get out of control.

Every year or two, we run into a client who calls our office every day and sometimes multiple times each day just to get an update on her case. We understand that the litigation process can be intimidating and scary, and we do our best to make sure every client understands the process and what we are doing every step of the way. But no matter how hard we work, the process takes time. Often, it can be weeks between events, and during that time, there is nothing to report to the client. It is important to understand that while you have the power to make the important decisions in your case, those choices only come up periodically. Between them are significant periods of downtime.

If you've done your homework and selected a lawyer you can trust, you need to let her do her job, understanding that when the time comes for you to make a decision, she will reach out to you, explain the possible options, and advise you on the best course of action.

Calling your lawyer every day does nothing to advance your claim, and it may actually hinder the lawyer's ability to do her best work on your case.

THE RIGHT ADVICE FROM THE RIGHT PEOPLE

One of the decisions you will need to make is what kind of medical treatment to get and for how long. This decision can be one of the most important of your case. Of course, the most important reason to make good treatment decisions is that you want to get better as quickly and completely as possible. This is your body we're talking about, and you will need to live in it for the rest of your life. If there is a treatment or procedure that can heal your injuries more completely or more permanently, you should do it not for any reason related to your case, but because getting better should always be your primary concern.

As a lawyer, I can tell you how certain kinds of treatment from certain types of providers can affect your case, but I can't tell you what kind of treatment to get. Despite this, I get calls from clients all the time saying something like: "I'm still getting shooting pains down my leg and my doctor thinks I should see a specialist. What should I do?" or "I'm doing physical therapy, but every time I move my neck a certain way, I get dizzy. What should I do?" My answer is always the same. Tell your doctor what is happening and follow his advice. If you don't like your doctor's advice, get a second opinion.

You get legal advice from your lawyer. You get medical advice from a doctor, and in both cases, you have to make the decisions that are best for you. From a legal point of view, I can tell you that if you've been getting the same kind of treatment for months and you aren't getting better, you should try something else. I can tell you that if you are having new or worsened symptoms, you have to tell your doctor about it. If you don't report your symptoms, they don't make it into your records, so it becomes difficult if not impossible for me to prove the extent of your injuries at trial. But I cannot tell you what kind of treatment you should be getting for your injuries.

RECOVERING THE VALUE OF YOUR VEHICLE

When a client hires me, it is to get a recovery for his injuries. But sometimes the primary concern, especially right after the accident, is getting his car repaired or replaced. It can be extremely frustrating when you need a car to get to work or take care of your kids, and your car is still in the shop, or even worse, is a total loss. What can you do?

The first thing you can do is get a rental car. When your car is wrecked by a negligent driver, the driver's insurance is required to provide you with a rental car until your car is repaired or until it can make a total loss offer. Usually, there's no problem getting a rental car, but if the insurance company balks at providing one, your attorney should be able to help. If you don't need a rental car, either because you have an extra vehicle, or because you were able to borrow one from a friend or family member, you are still entitled to a "loss of use" payment for the time you don't have your car. This is usually an amount equivalent to the cost of renting a small car.

If your car can be fixed, you can either go through your own collision coverage or the other driver's liability coverage. The disadvantage of using your own insurance is that there's usually a deductible, or an amount you have to pay out-of-pocket, but in a case of clear liability, your insurance will sometimes waive the deductible and recover it directly from the other insurance.

Whether you go through your own insurance or that of the other driver, the procedure is generally the same. Usually, the insurance company will send a property damage adjuster to inspect your car and prepare a repair estimate. Once you get the estimate, you take your car to an approved shop, which works directly with the insurance company. First, the shop prepares a preliminary repair estimate and the insurance pays for that. In almost every case, once the shop starts working on your car, it discovers additional damage, and it prepares supplemental invoices for the insurance company to pay. The advantage of using an approved shop is that the repairs are usually guaranteed for life. That means if the paint starts peeling or the new bumper falls off, the shop will stand by its work and fix the repair.

If your car is a total loss, things can be a bit more complicated. As I said above, you get a rental car or loss of use payment until the insurance company makes an offer for the value of your car. However, once the offer is made, even if you don't accept it, you only have a few more days of rental car coverage. The offers are not based on blue book or on asking price, but rather on a comprehensive database of actual sales of comparable vehicles within a specific geographic area. While you are certainly allowed to negotiate this amount, it can be difficult to increase the total loss offer.

One of the things you can do to increase the offer is to document substantial aftermarket additions or recent major repairs, such as an engine replacement. Sometimes even documenting that the tires were recently replaced can increase the insurance company's offer. Again, most attorneys primarily deal with the bodily injury portion of the claim, but a good lawyer will help facilitate the resolution of your property damage claim as well, and he or she will provide you with strategies to maximize your recovery for your damaged or totaled car.

CONCLUSION

An attorney is an expert in advising you in the aftermath of an accident, freeing you to focus on your treatment and on taking care of your family. But merely hiring a lawyer does not relieve you of any responsibility for your case. The big decisions are still yours, only now you have a dedicated and highly qualified advisor to help you make the right decisions. Remember, lawyers are good for giving legal advice, but don't look to your lawyer for medical advice. For that, you need to rely on your doctors. Usually, the lawyer's advice will be right on the mark, but occasionally, you may decide to go a different way. That is your right, and as long as you maintain good communication with your lawyer, he should be able to support your decisions and work with you to achieve the desired outcome. Even with the best lawyer, your claim will almost certainly have complications. The next chapter discusses some of those complications, how you can anticipate them, and in some cases, avoid them entirely.

CHAPTER 11

DEALING WITH COMPLICATIONS

*I'm full of fears and I do my best to avoid difficulties and
any kind of complications. I like everything around
me to be clear as crystal and completely calm.*

— Alfred Hitchcock

In the previous chapter, I talked about your right and responsibility to make the major decisions in your case, hopefully with the assistance and advice of a good attorney. In this chapter, I discuss various things that can go wrong with your case, many of which are completely out of your control. What do you do if there are multiple accidents, or multiple vehicles involved in the accident? How is the case changed if you had injuries or medical conditions before the accident? What if you have to move to another state or country while your case is pending? What if the insurance company and its lawyers view your social media accounts? None of these situations necessarily prevent you from making a full financial recovery for your injuries, but each presents complications that need to be dealt with. Ignoring these issues could result in a significant reduction in your financial recovery.

FOUR DEFENDANTS, TWO ACCIDENTS, ONE CASE

In November, 2010, Enrique Flores was riding as a passenger in his girlfriend's car. As they were driving down the freeway, his girlfriend failed to realize until too late that the lane she was using was about to end. Because of heavy traffic, she was unable to merge into the adjacent lane, so she put her turn signal on and came to a stop. Suddenly, her car was rear-ended by the car behind hers. A few seconds later, the car was hit again by another following car.

Enrique immediately felt pain in his neck and back, and after consulting with his doctor, he began a course of treatment, including physical therapy and massage. After several months of treatment, Enrique was improving, but he was still having pain in his back. Unfortunately, before he was completely healed, he was involved in another accident. Again, he was a passenger in his girlfriend's car when another car backed into them in a parking lot. Enrique's neck and back were aggravated by this accident, and he suffered a new injury to his shoulder. Enrique returned to his doctor and began a new course of treatment for his injuries.

Eventually, Enrique completed his treatment, and his injuries, while not completely resolved, become only a minor annoyance. We were ready to move forward with his claim. But who was the claim against? Could we accurately separate the injuries from the two accidents? Was the first accident his girlfriend's fault for not realizing that the lane was about to end? Which one of the following cars was responsible? In a situation like this, it can be impossible to know who is ultimately responsible for the damage caused. Fortunately, Enrique had hired us and we knew how to handle this situation.

We prepared a comprehensive demand package detailing the facts of both accidents, all of Enrique's injuries, and all of his medical treatment. We sent this package to the insurance companies for every driver involved in these two incidents. Fortunately for Enrique, he was a passenger in both accidents, so there could be no claim that he was in any way responsible for either crash. Usually in a case like this, the insurance companies are able to reach some kind of agreement regarding the apportionment of the damages, so all that is left for me and my client is to establish the value of his damages. In this case, every defendant and his or her insurance company denied liability. Each one pointed the finger at the others.

Ultimately, in this case, we had no choice but to file a lawsuit against all of the defendants, including Enrique's girlfriend. We explained to him that we did not believe she was responsible, but as long as the other defendants were pointing the finger at her, it was important to have her as part of the lawsuit, and her insurance company would hire a lawyer to defend her. Fortunately for Enrique, his girlfriend understood the situation and supported his decision.

In the months leading to the arbitration of this claim, none of the defendants would budge. Each asserted he or she was completely fault free. Enrique really didn't care who was found to be responsible as long as he was compensated for his loss. We presented the case to an arbitrator, focusing mostly on Enrique's injuries, wage loss, and the impact the injuries had on his life. We let the defendants fight it out among themselves to establish who was at fault. After a day-long hearing, the arbitrator ruled that the car directly behind Enrique's vehicle was 100 percent responsible for the first accident and he awarded damages for Enrique's injuries. Enrique was further awarded damages from the driver in the second incident in the parking lot.

It took a lot of work, and more than a year, but we finally got Enrique a full recovery for his injuries. Even though he was completely without fault for these incidents, the claim was very complicated because of the number of people and insurance companies involved. It is unlikely he would have been able to recover anything without the help of an attorney.

THE EGGSHELL PLAINTIFF

Even when there is only one accident with one defendant, a simple claim can be complicated by a prior condition. Peter Bostwick had advanced rheumatoid arthritis when he was T-boned by a car pulling out of a driveway. The impact was relatively minor, and it possibly wouldn't have caused significant injury to someone who was healthy. But for Peter, the injuries were devastating. The pain in his neck and back was unbearable. He was confined to his bed for an extended period, and he required several months of aggressive treatment just to restore some of the function he had before the accident.

When Peter attempted to resolve his claim with the insurance company, it told him that all of his problems were from his pre-existing condition, and it refused to offer more than a few hundred dollars to make him go away.

This is a classic case of an "eggshell plaintiff." An eggshell plaintiff is a person who, for whatever reason, is more fragile and more susceptible to injury from an impact that might not injure a stronger or healthier person. A person could be more susceptible to injury for a number of reasons. It could be a chronic disease like rheumatoid arthritis or diabetes. It could be a prior injury or prior surgery. It could be as simple as old age. What distinguishes cases like these is that because of a person's particular circumstance, he or she is more likely to be injured—sometimes severely injured—than a typical person. The reaction of the insurance company to Peter's claim was pretty typical and absolutely predictable. It was looking for any reason to reduce what it had to pay him, or even better, to avoid paying at all. The burden was on Peter and me, his lawyer, to prove that the injuries were related to the accident and to make the insurance company pay.

In Peter's case, the most important thing was to give him time and space to recover from his injuries. I contacted the insurance company and advised it to back off while Peter was recovering. I instructed it to direct any questions or concerns it had to my office and not to make any further attempt to speak with my client. This is often an important step in helping clients heal from their injuries. The stress of dealing with the insurance company can be overwhelming and can actually interfere with your body's ability to heal. By creating a buffer between my clients and insurance companies, I give my clients the time and space they need to heal in peace, care for their families, and begin to restore their lives to normal.

As Peter recovered, we began to speak to his doctors, discuss how his prior condition made him more susceptible to injury from this accident, and attempt to determine which injuries were new and which were aggravations of his prior condition. We persuaded several of his doctors to write detailed reports regarding Peter's condition, and we included those reports with his medical records when we submitted a demand for settlement to the insurance company.

Even with the reports in hand, the insurance company balked at paying the claim. It continued to assert that it could blame all of Peter's problems on his pre-existing condition and that a jury would rule in its favor. We filed a lawsuit and began to move toward trial. Before we got there, the insurance company invited us to participate in a mediation of the claim. Mediation is a form of facilitated negotiation and will be discussed in more detail later. We agreed to the mediation, and ultimately, we were able to settle the claim. One of the things about mediation is we don't get to hear what the mediator is saying to the insurance company's adjusters and attorneys, but in this case, he must have persuaded them that it would be foolish to try to blame all of Peter's problems on his arthritis because the insurance company ended up offering all of his accident-related medical bills plus a significant amount for his pain and suffering and other non-economic damages.

This case should have been simple, but because of the complicating factor of Peter's pre-existing condition, it took almost two years and lots of legal maneuvering to get Peter a fair recovery.

DO YOU HAVE A PUNCH CARD?

One of the problems I occasionally run into is the person who has been in multiple car accidents in the past, often with exactly the same injuries as he has now. The insurance companies love these situations because they give them an opportunity to blame all of the person's current problems on the prior accidents and to deny any responsibility for the current injuries.

Diana Halberg was one of my first clients. She experienced a simple rear-end car accident with some mild neck and back whiplash, and we were able to get her a fair settlement. Since then, she's been back with four separate claims. None of these claims were her fault, and they were all real. In one case, she slipped on a defective wheelchair ramp and broke her leg. In another, some heavy merchandise fell from a store shelf onto her head. Then there were the car accidents. Each of these incidents caused injury, and each required medical treatment.

When Diana called me last year with a new car accident claim, I was concerned. With so many prior accidents, how would we get the insurance company to pay for the damage its driver caused in this most recent accident? Diana acknowledged the problem and asked whether I could start a punch card for her—"Tenth case is free."

Diana's situation is kind of like a combination of the first two examples. Although I was representing her for only one accident, the insurance company could try to blame several other incidents for the injuries just like it did in Enrique's case. And although Diana did not have a chronic illness like Peter, the multiple prior injuries left her with chronic pain and made her more susceptible to a serious injury from the next accident.

In cases like this one, it can actually help to use the same doctors you've used in the past. Because these providers have treated you through multiple injuries, they have a baseline for you. They know what your injuries were from each accident and how well they resolved. They know what your underlying level of wellness was before the most recent accident.

Fortunately for Diana, she used the same chiropractor after all of her accidents. Of course, she had other providers as well, but the chiropractor provided a constant through all of her treatment. At the conclusion of each case, he had documented which injuries had resolved and which would be permanent. We used his records, as well as a detailed report from him, to establish which injuries were new from this most recent accident and which were aggravations of prior conditions. Ultimately, with the support of Diana's doctor, we were able to negotiate a very fair settlement for her despite the multiple prior injuries that had the potential to derail her claim.

At the end of the case, I did make up a punch card for Diana and punched out the first five holes. I hope she'll never need my services again, but if she does, I know we'll be able to prove what her physical condition was before the accident, and what injuries were caused by the next accident.

THE SOCIAL MEDIA TRAP

If you're like me, you love social media: Facebook, Twitter, Instagram, Vine, Foursquare, Google Plus. You name it and I've probably posted there in the last twenty-four hours. Social media is a great way to stay in touch with friends, engage in community or political activism, discuss current events, and share thoughts and ideas. It is also one of the tools the insurance company will try to use to defeat your injury claim.

Your social media accounts can be used against you in multiple ways. First, the insurance company can use your posts about everyday activities to suggest to the jury that you really weren't that badly hurt. Of course, you aren't going to stop picking up your baby just because your lower back hurts, but you can bet the insurance company will make the most of it. Just putting a picture in front of the jury of you lifting your child creates doubt about your injury and raises the suggestion that you are exaggerating or even faking your injuries and your doctors are all frauds. Of course, the jury won't really believe that, but the insurance company lawyers don't have to *prove* anything. All they have to do is create confusion and doubt and they win.

Another potential hazard of social media arises when you actually do engage in strenuous or risky activities while you are getting treatment for your injuries. Perhaps you had a vacation to Cabo scheduled months in advance, and while there, you decided to try windsurfing or paddle boarding. Perhaps you were at the park and were tackled by a St. Bernard. If you post photos of these activities on your social media accounts, there is a good chance the insurance company will find them and try to use them against you. While there are explanations for such activities, my experience is that the more you have to explain at trial, the worse your chances are of getting a fair recovery.

Sometimes a condition of settling a claim is a confidentiality agreement. This means that you will agree to refrain from making public statements about the incident, the other party, and your settlement.

If you use your social media accounts to discuss the incident or to badmouth the other party, this could negatively impact your ability to resolve your claim.

If you have a pending injury claim, my advice is to suspend your social media accounts immediately. Do not post anything and do not let other people post to your profiles. Cancel the accounts if possible. If you are simply unwilling to do this, at least change your privacy settings to maximize your privacy. Be aware, however, that some courts have ruled your social media accounts are not private and you may be forced to disclose them to the insurance company lawyers if you proceed to trial.

A good rule of thumb is to consider that anything you post can and probably will be used against you. Use social media with extreme caution. Better yet, for the duration of your case, don't use it at all.

CONCLUSION

Many complicating factors can make it difficult for you to get a full recovery for your claim. Often, the insurance company will pounce on these complications and try to use them as justification for reducing your settlement or even refusing to make any offer at all. However troublesome these complications may seem, they are often nothing more than minor bumps in the road if handled properly. Use the next few lines to write down some of the issues you worry might complicate your case. Then, share them with your lawyer. If they are real problems, your attorney will let you know, but usually it will be a simple matter for a good lawyer to anticipate any problems these issues might cause and deal with them efficiently. This way, you can focus your energy on the important stuff, like getting better and getting your life back to normal. _____
_____
_____

CHAPTER 12
SHIELDING YOU FROM THE CHAOS

The battlefield is a scene of constant chaos. The winner will be the one who controls that chaos, both his own and the enemy's.

— Napoleon Bonaparte

In the previous chapter, I talked about the kinds of issues that can complicate your claim. In that chapter, we addressed how a good attorney can often minimize the impact of those issues, or even eliminate them altogether, freeing you to focus your attention on your recovery and your family. However, even if there are no particular complicating issues, the process of personal injury claims and litigation, in particular, can be difficult and stressful. Long periods of downtime can occur in which nothing seems to happen, followed by furious flurries of activity. Rude and aggressive claims adjusters and attorneys may need to be dealt with. Often, multiple insurance companies are arguing over who should pay. If you try to handle all of this yourself, you could easily become overwhelmed and discouraged. In this chapter, I will discuss some of the chaos that results from the uncertainty of the personal injury claims process and how having the right attorney can protect you from the worst of these situations, providing you with peace of mind.

THE DANDELION CHALLENGE

As a homeowner with a reasonably large backyard, weeds have become my enemy. I am constantly dealing with infestations of clover, dandelions, and other weeds that threaten to overtake my beautiful green lawn. But as a kid, I didn't know anything about weeds. Dandelions were just pretty yellow flowers. I liked to pick them and give them to my mom, and when they became puffballs, I liked to blow the seeds into the wind and make a wish.

Occasionally, as I was growing up in the New York City suburbs, we would visit my grandparents in Upper Greenwood Lake, near West Milford, New Jersey. They had a beautiful house just up the hill from the lake. During the winters, the lake would freeze over, and we could skate on it. At other times of the year, the landscape was lush and green. During these warmer seasons, my grandparents' yard would frequently become overrun with dandelions.

Often during our visits, my grandfather would offer my sister and me a penny for every dandelion we could pick. He'd give us work gloves and buckets and send us out into the very large yard. We'd spend hours in the yard running around and playing. We'd roll down hills and climb trees. In between, we'd joyfully pluck dandelions from the grass and place them in our buckets. There weren't many other kids in the neighborhood, but the dandelion challenge kept us occupied for a good part of the day. After a while, dirty and exhausted, we'd trudge back to the house with our buckets overflowing with weeds. Then he'd sit us down to count what we had picked. We would carefully count each dandelion until we knew we had it right, and my grandfather would happily hand over a few dollars to both of us.

Even now, I have fond memories of picking dandelions in my grandparents' yard, but as an adult and a parent, I have a deeper understanding of what was happening. On a surface level, my grandfather wanted to get rid of the weeds in his yard, and hiring us was a cheap and easy way to do it. I'm sure he enjoyed looking out his kitchen window at a green lawn without any dandelions on it. But I don't think he really cared that much about getting rid of the weeds. As an adult, I can see that he was encouraging our work ethic and teaching us the value of money, but I have no doubt that he was also trying to get us out of the house so the grownups could discuss serious issues without upsetting us. Or maybe it was just to give them a break from the craziness of little kids. Either way, it worked. We were happy, we earned some money, and they got to deal with the serious issues of life without burdening our minds with things we couldn't control. To this day, I'm grateful to my grandfather for encouraging and protecting us in this way and letting us enjoy our visits to the country.

Managing a personal injury claim is like taking care of a big green lawn. Weeds often pop up when you least expect them, and there are issues that need to be dealt with every day. And while a personal injury client is certainly not a child, and he has a right to know what is happening in his case, he does not need to be burdened with every rude phone call from a claims adjuster, every threat to close a file, every dispute over liability and damages, and every refusal to pay.

I believe my clients' energies are best spent on healing their physical and emotional injuries, and on spending time at their jobs and with their families, not worrying over a rude defense attorney. I create a protective bubble around my clients, insulating them from the day-to-day bothers of their claim. Of course, I keep them informed of all significant developments and make sure they are empowered to make all of the major decisions about their case, but I believe one of the biggest benefits of hiring a lawyer is to shield you from the stress and unpleasantness of the day-to-day management of your case.

WHY YOU GOTTA BE SO RUDE?

I believe in being a strong and aggressive advocate for my clients. I believe that injured people deserve to be compensated for their injuries and the effect on their lives, and I am prepared to use the full extent of the law to obtain a complete recovery for my clients. But there is a big and important difference between being aggressive and being unprofessional. I always conduct myself with professionalism and courtesy to everyone involved in my clients' claims. This professionalism starts with my clients themselves, and extends to their families, their doctors, as well as the insurance personnel and the opposing attorney. While I have found that most attorneys share this value and attempt to treat me and my clients with courtesy and respect even while disputing the claim, some claims adjusters and attorneys are consistently rude and antagonistic for no good reason. Perhaps they think being rude will intimidate me. Perhaps they think that to be a good advocate, they have to be insulting and dismissive of the other side, making demands and threats without regard for the other side's needs. In my experience, claims adjusters and attorneys like this are doing their clients a great disservice and making a favorable outcome less likely.

One of the areas where I most often run into rudeness is scheduling. When a client's PIP coverage is paying her medical bills, the policy allows the insurance carrier to request an independent medical exam or IME. I call these "insurance medical exams" because there's really nothing independent about them. In an IME, the insurance company requires you to be examined by a doctor of its choosing to obtain an opinion about whether it should continue paying for your medical treatment. Obviously, the doctors the insurance companies continue to use are the ones who give the opinions the insurance companies want. Regardless of the problems with this process, if you are getting your medical bills paid with your PIP coverage, your policy almost certainly requires that you comply with the request to attend an IME. Most of the time, the claims adjuster will contact my office to arrange a mutually convenient time and place for the IME, but occasionally, I get a threatening letter informing me that an IME has been set for a specific date and place, and if my client fails to attend, he will be in violation of the policy.

This situation is one where I believe it is best to protect my client from the potential fear and anxiety that might come from such a threat. I inform the adjuster that my client has every intention of cooperating with the terms of the policy, but he will do it at a time and place that will work for him. I then make sure I find a date and location that is convenient for my client, and I facilitate the examination.

Another situation comes up with defense attorneys who are always yelling and making threats on the phone. These lawyers will unilaterally set deadlines, make threats, and then follow up the call with a letter falsely claiming we agreed to something. This requires a follow-up letter clarifying that we never agreed to anything, which often prompts an angry response. This kind of litigation is extremely stressful, and it doesn't lead to anything good except occasionally getting a judge involved, who is usually just as annoyed as we are by the whole process. In situations like this, I refuse to speak to the opposing attorney by phone, requiring all communications to be in writing to avoid any further "misunderstandings."

Hundreds of different situations can occur in which a hospital billing department, health insurance agent, claims representative, or opposing attorney can be rude or inappropriately aggressive, attempting to bully or intimidate. An injured person really shouldn't have to deal with these situations. By having a qualified attorney involved from early in the process, you can protect yourself from this nonsense, while making sure that your claim is being handled properly.

WHY WON'T YOU PAY MY BILLS?

Sometimes an issue is as simple as figuring out which of several insurance companies has to pay your medical bills, but it can be a nightmare dealing with the representatives of several different insurance companies, each claiming that it is not its responsibility to pay. For example, Juliette Bacardi was riding in a commercial shuttle bus that was struck by another car. Juliette had health insurance and personal injury protection coverage (PIP) through her auto insurance. The shuttle bus had MedPay coverage, which is very similar to PIP coverage. The car that struck the bus also had PIP coverage. Who was responsible to pay Juliette's medical bills?

While Juliette was trying to figure this out, and each of the insurance companies was denying responsibility to pay, bills for thousands of dollars were being sent to her. If she didn't act fast, all of these bills would end up in collections, ruining her credit for years. She was in extreme pain, unable to work as a hair stylist, and trying to make it to her appointments and get better. The last thing she needed was an argument with four different insurance companies.

Fortunately, Juliette called me and I took her case. The first thing I did was speak to each insurance company to find out exactly why it believed the bills were not its responsibility. Then I asked for copies of the policies, and specifically what language in the policies relieved each company of the duty to pay. Ultimately, it became clear that the primary insurance was the MedPay for the shuttle bus. Once that was exhausted (which it rapidly was), Juliette's own PIP coverage was next in line. Finally, if Juliette's PIP was exhausted or denied for any reason, her health insurance would take over. Once I got this mess sorted out, Juliette's bills were paid right away and the threat of collections, along with the stress created by it, disappeared.

When you hire a lawyer, one of the first things he should do is figure out what is your most immediate concern. Often, if the lawyer is hired shortly after the accident, the biggest concern is getting the car fixed or replaced. Sometimes, as in Juliette's case, it is figuring out who should be paying the bills and making sure they get paid. Whatever it is, your primary concern should be getting better. If you are distracted by anything else, you are diminishing your body's ability to heal, and you are creating unnecessary stress for yourself and your family.

I'VE GOT THIS

Every once in awhile, I get a client who is so used to taking care of things himself that he can't let go. This situation can be counterproductive for a couple of reasons. First, as we've already discussed, when you are spending all of your time dealing with insurance companies and trying to figure out what to do and say at every turn, you have less energy to focus on your recovery and your family. It is the full-time job of the people on the other side of your claim to make sure you don't get fair compensation, and they are generally pretty good at it. Even if you have all the time in the world, you are going up against pros, and it will be difficult and likely stressful to deal with them yourself. Second, in addition to the potential stress from dealing with the insurance companies, you could actually harm your claim or place yourself in a more difficult situation by trying to deal with it yourself.

Arnold Brighton broke his leg when a car struck him in a parking lot. The driver who hit him had PIP coverage. Arnold had PIP coverage of his own, and he had health insurance. Until it could be sorted out which insurance company would pay the bills, the providers were left with outstanding balances. Although they agreed to wait to be paid until we sorted out the insurance situation, they continued sending bills to Arnold.

When Arnold hired me, I told him, as I tell all of my clients, to let me take care of everything. I told him that if he were worried about anything other than healing his broken leg, then I wasn't doing my job, and that the reason he hired a lawyer was to make the process easier. I specifically told him that anytime he got a bill, a collection notice, or any correspondence related to his medical bills, he should immediately send it to me so my office could deal with it appropriately. He said he understood, but when the bills started arriving in his mailbox, he was either unable or unwilling to let my office take care of them.

Arnold repeatedly called the billing offices for the ambulance company, the hospital, and the surgeons. He called his health insurance and his auto insurance. He was angry and frustrated, and he wanted to know why he was being billed instead of having one of the insurance companies take care of the bills. When a person is injured and medicated, he might sometimes speak without thinking, and Arnold could easily have made a statement to the insurance company that could have compromised his claim. Fortunately, I had sent letters of representation to all of the involved insurance companies instructing them that they were not authorized to speak with my client. Ultimately, it was Arnold's auto insurance company that contacted me and advised me that he was repeatedly calling the claims adjuster.

I reached out to Arnold and had a long conversation with him. It turns out he had always managed his family's finances and he was uncomfortable having unpaid bills out there. I reassured him that I would take care of it, and I promised that I would keep him in the loop. He sent me all of the bills, and I immediately contacted all of the billing offices and assured them that the bills would be taken care of. I then coordinated with the various insurance companies and established which would be paying. I reached out to Arnold each day and let him know what I had discovered. Within a few days, the insurance companies had agreed to pay, and within a week, the bills started to get paid. The billing departments were happy, and, most importantly, Arnold was happy.

Even if you're used to taking care of everything yourself, it is definitely in your interest after you hire a lawyer to let the lawyer do the work you hired him to do. If you need to be more involved, let your lawyer know; then she should keep you included in the process. In the end, letting your lawyer do the job she was hired to do will be better for you and better for your claim.

CONCLUSION

A personal injury claim can be complex and labor intensive. From the day of your accident, issues arise involving health care, insurance, police, and more. You will be asked to give statements to the police and various insurance companies. You will need to get your car repaired or replaced, and you may need a rental car. While you are getting treatment for your injuries, the insurance company will want to rush you into a settlement and may even bully you. Once your treatment ends and negotiations start, the people you are dealing with can be professional and efficient, but they can also be rude and aggressive. At every step of this process, it is in your best interest to have an attorney protecting your rights and acting as your advocate. When you hire an attorney, you do not give up any control over your case or your situation. You remain in charge. You just have someone to handle the day-to-day ugliness inherent in the process. Letting your attorney do her job will be one of the best decisions you can make. Even if you follow your lawyer's lead, dealing with the insurance company can be time-consuming and frustrating. The next chapter will address some of the things insurance companies may ask you to do before you can resolve your claim.

CHAPTER 13
JUMPING THROUGH INSURANCE COMPANY HOOPS

Passion is a huge prerequisite to winning. It makes you willing to jump through hoops, go through all the ups and downs and everything in between to reach your goal."

— Kerri Walsh, Olympic Gold Medalist in Beach Volleyball

In the last chapter, we discussed the benefits of letting your attorney handle the day-to-day issues that inevitably come up in your case. But there are always things you will need to do to keep your case moving forward. A good attorney will do what he can to keep your case on the right track, and he will let you know when there is something you need to do yourself. In this chapter, I will discuss some of those things that the insurance companies require you to do as part of your claim. These tasks can include answering questions in writing or in person, disclosing information about yourself, and even submitting to an examination by a doctor chosen by the insurance company. Failure to comply with these requests could significantly harm your claim, or even prevent you from getting a recovery at all.

PAPERWORK, PAPERWORK

You've been paying your auto insurance and health insurance premiums for years. These policies provide that if you need medical treatment, it will be paid for. So, now that you've been injured in an accident and you need treatment, the insurance company is paying all of your bills, right? Well, maybe but probably not. Before either your personal injury protection (PIP) or your health insurance will pay your medical bills following an accident, they almost always require written documents to be completed and signed by you.

If you have PIP coverage, that is primary over your health insurance. That means your PIP will pay all of your bills first until your coverage is exhausted or denied. At that point, your health insurance steps in and takes over payments. But before your PIP will pay your bills, the insurance company usually requires a written application for PIP benefits. This application often asks for detailed information about how the accident happened, what injuries you sustained, and what treatment, if any, you have received so far. It usually also asks about any wage loss you have sustained, and any prior injuries you have that may have contributed to your condition. Finally, the PIP application includes an authorization for the release of medical records. By completing this form, you are giving the insurance company permission to see your medical records and the medical treatment it is paying for, but it is vital to make sure this authorization is limited to the PIP carrier and does not give the liability carrier or anyone else permission to view your medical records.

It is important to fill out these forms carefully. While you want to be accurate, you do not want to give the insurance company an unnecessary reason to question or deny your payments. I generally recommend that my client either fill out the forms and send them to me for review before sending them in to the insurance company, or even better, let me fill them out with the information he has provided to me; then I have the client sign the form for me to send in. By doing this, I insure that all of the required information is provided without saying anything that could compromise the case.

Once the PIP is exhausted, or if there is no PIP coverage, your health insurance becomes primary. Health insurance will pay the bills, pursuant to the terms of your policy, whether your injuries are accident-related or not, but if the treatment is accident-related and you are making a claim against a third-party, your insurance company may have a right of subrogation. Subrogation means the insurance company gets paid back a portion of what it paid out of your final recovery. In order to determine whether it has a right of subrogation, your health insurance company might send an accident questionnaire. This document asks for specific information about the accident and the injuries it caused, as well as information about the person who caused the accident and his or her auto insurance company. Sometimes, your health insurance company will use this information to file a lien. A lien is a legal document that serves as a general notice that it is owed money from your claim. Once a lien is filed, your lawyer has a legal obligation to make sure it gets paid back out of your settlement. Usually, though, instead of filing a lien, your health insurance company simply notifies your attorney of its subrogation interest and begins processing and paying for your accident-related treatment.

As with the application for PIP benefits, the accident questionnaire contains many questions, and in answering them, it would be easy to provide unnecessary or irrelevant information, which could adversely affect your claim. In order to make sure your interests are protected, it's a good idea to have this form reviewed by an attorney before it is sent in to the insurance company.

THE RECORDED STATEMENT

Once you file a lawsuit, the third-party liability insurer, through its attorney, can require you to attend a deposition. I will address the deposition in a later chapter, but it is essentially an opportunity for the insurance company's attorney to ask you questions under oath. Except in very unusual circumstances, there is no right to a deposition before a lawsuit has been filed, but the insurance company can request a recorded statement, and it can make it a condition of settlement. While you have no legal obligation to cooperate or give a statement to the other person's insurance, it is often in your best interest to do so, as long as you know what you are doing and you are represented by an attorney.

Very often, the liability insurer will attempt to contact you shortly after the accident to obtain a recorded statement. It will often tell you that such a statement is required, and that it will not move its investigation forward unless you agree to give a statement. I have heard horror stories from clients that insurance adjusters contacted them in their hospital rooms, shortly after surgery, when they are on high doses of pain medication and can barely think straight. I have seen other examples where the adjuster twists the injured person's words, trying to shift fault for the accident or to minimize the injuries. This is a critical time in your claim, and you need to understand that the adjuster is aggressively looking for ways to reduce the compensation the insurance company will pay, even if he seems like he is being nice.

You should never, ever give a statement to the liability insurance company without an attorney unless you have decided to try to resolve the claim on your own. Even then, you need to make sure you are at your best—fully alert and not distracted or impaired by pain, medication, or anything else. If you decide to give a statement, you should pay careful attention to the words the adjuster is using, and you should answer only the questions asked as precisely as you can.

Often when clients hire me, they have already given a statement to the insurance company. In those cases, I immediately get a copy of the statement and make sure everything that was said was accurate and that nothing can be misconstrued or taken out of context. Usually, nothing devastating is said in those statements, but sometimes, a misunderstanding needs to be corrected right away.

In one claim, my client Lauren Tibbs kept referring to the pain in her arm as a prior injury. She meant her arm was injured in the auto accident prior to the recorded statement, but her meaning was not clear. The claims adjuster took advantage of this misunderstanding and tried to make a record that the arm pain pre-existed the accident. Upon reviewing the recording and discussing it with Lauren, I was able to correct the record before it could do any harm.

The best recommendation I can give is that if the liability insurer requests a recorded statement, you should decline, even if it threatens to close the file. Without an attorney present to protect your rights and prevent the adjuster from intimidating or threatening you, too many things can easily go wrong and create misunderstandings. Sometimes, I do allow the insurance company to take a statement from my client if I think it will help move the claim forward, but only under specific circumstances and with an attorney present. This hoop is just one of many we sometimes need to jump through in order to get your claim resolved.

PRIOR RECORDS

Sometimes, even after we have provided the liability insurer with all of your relevant medical records and bills, it will refuse to extend an offer of settlement without seeing your prior records as well. In one respect, this request is legitimate and makes sense. If we are claiming damages for an injured wrist, the liability insurer has a right to make sure you didn't have an injury to that wrist before the accident. If you did, even if that injury was aggravated in the accident, you only have a right to be compensated for the worsening of the injury, not for the whole injury.

Unfortunately, as with most things, the insurance companies usually overreach in requesting prior records. I've seen insurance companies request all of your prior records from every provider you've seen in the last ten years and sometimes even longer. Such a request is absurd. It's grossly overbroad, and it is designed to allow the insurance company to go on a "fishing expedition" where it can scour your records looking for any reason to reduce your recovery. I do not allow such an expedition, and I discourage everyone from providing unlimited medical authorizations to the insurance company. Instead, if the circumstances warrant, I will advise my client to agree to provide the insurance company with relevant records, that is records of injuries or treatments similar to those claimed to result from the accident, for a period no longer than five years prior to the accident.

Even with such a limitation, obtaining and providing prior medical records is a hassle. It can add expenses to your claim, and it can delay an offer often by several months or more. I do not provide prior records in every case—only where such records would be relevant. I also don't allow the insurance company to obtain those records on its own. Instead, I obtain the records first to make sure they are relevant before I provide them to the other side. This is just one of the many hoops the insurance company can make us jump through before I can obtain a financial recovery for you.

THE INSURANCE MEDICAL EXAMINATION

In a previous chapter, I mentioned the "Independent Medical Examination" or IME. I prefer to call this the "insurance medical examination" because there is really nothing "independent" about it. The insurance company selects a doctor to examine you in order to cut off payments for your medical treatment or to prove that your treatment was either unreasonable or not accident-related at trial. In either case, the insurance company selects doctors who are most likely to give the opinion it wants. And because many of these doctors make significant portions of their incomes from doing these insurance exams, you can be sure they are motivated to give the opinion the insurance company wants. In my experience, less than 5 percent of these examinations are favorable to my clients. Fortunately, most judges and arbitrators understand how this system works and give the opinions of these doctors less weight than your treating doctors. Unfortunately, the IME is still a hoop that you will probably have to jump through to move your case forward.

Two distinct situations exist in which you might need to attend an IME. The first is when you are using your own PIP coverage to pay for your accident-related medical treatment. The second is after a lawsuit has been filed and you are making a claim for ongoing pain, disability, or other problems as a result of the accident. In each situation, you can be required to provide the examining doctor with your prior medical records, give a history of the accident and your injuries, and submit to a comprehensive physical examination. Within a week or so, the examiner will issue a report stating (in his opinion) whether you really were injured, whether the injuries are accident-related, whether the treatment you received was appropriate, and whether you continue to have any problems related to the accident. The insurance company or its attorney will rely on this report to try to pay less for your treatment or to reduce your award at trial. A good attorney will know how to respond to this report and help increase the odds that you will get what you deserve.

The PIP IME

The first example we will discuss is the PIP IME. In this situation, you are receiving payments for your accident-related medical bills from your own auto insurance. If you have PIP coverage, your insurer is required to pay for all reasonable, medically necessary, and accident-related treatment. As discussed in a previous chapter, the advantages of PIP coverage are that there is no deductible or co-pay, no network of providers, and no referral requirement. You can see any doctor you want, and the insurance must pay up to your limits as long as it meets the above requirements. One disadvantage of PIP coverage is that it requires your cooperation with the insurance company, including its right to investigate whether the treatment actually is reasonable, medically necessary, and accident-related.

Sometimes your insurance company will try to deny payments based on a review of your medical records alone. Courts are divided on this issue, but I believe a mere records review is not a sufficient investigation to overrule the opinions of your treating doctors. Instead, if the insurance company wants to cut off your payments, it must have a medical opinion that the treatment does not meet the policy's requirements. This opinion is obtained through an IME. Once your insurance company requests an IME, it is your duty to comply within a reasonable time. Although it's never convenient to attend an IME, I work with the insurance companies to set up a time and place that is least inconvenient for my client. In particularly contentious cases, I will send a nurse or another health care professional to attend the IME as a witness.

Before you ever arrive at the IME, I make sure the examining doctor has a copy of your treatment records. Once you arrive, the exam usually starts with a history. This is basically a question and answer period. It is essential that you remember this doctor is not there to treat you. He is not your doctor, and he is not looking out for your best interest. He is looking for ways to justify the insurance company cutting off payments for your treatment. Because of this arrangement, while you should always be honest, you should never be casual about what you say. You need to pay careful attention to what the doctor is asking and answer only the questions asked. You should refrain from giving your opinion about what caused your injuries. That is a medical opinion best left to the doctors. In the cases where I send a witness, she often records this portion of the exam to make sure the doctor does not change or exaggerate what is being said.

After the history is the physical examination. You should never, ever do anything during this exam that will cause you pain or aggravate your condition, but you should also not exaggerate your symptoms. Doctors (especially the ones who perform IMEs) are very sensitive to what they call "exaggerated pain behavior," and if they think you are exaggerating, they will surely count that against you. The physical exam could take anywhere from twenty minutes to an hour, and once it is finished, you are free to go.

It is important to note that in most cases, regardless of what you say and how the examination goes, the doctor will report to the insurance company that no further treatment is warranted. You should not be afraid of that outcome. It is, for the most part, to be expected, and it does not mean you can't continue your treatment. It just means that your auto insurance is going to try to get out of paying for it. Your auto policy probably has an arbitration clause that provides for dispute resolution if you disagree with your insurer's decision on your medical bills, but in most cases, this type of arbitration is not worth pursuing because other ways usually exist to get the bills paid, and you are ultimately seeking to recover your medical bills from the third-party insurer anyway.

The Third-Party IME

While your PIP coverage pays your medical bills as they are incurred, the third-party liability insurance only pays once, at the conclusion of your case, either through settlement or litigation. The PIP carrier requests an IME to cut off your medical payments while the liability carrier requests an IME to reduce or completely eliminate your recovery at arbitration or trial. While the PIP IME is required by your contract with your own insurer, the third-party IME is performed pursuant to court rules.

Washington Courts Civil Rule 35 provides in part:

> *When the mental or physical condition...of a party...is in controversy, the court in which the action is pending may order the party to submit to a physical examination by a physician, or mental examination by a physician or psychologist....*

Basically, what this rule says is that if you are claiming ongoing pain or disability as the result of an accident, the court may allow the defense to have a doctor of its choosing examine you. Such an exam is so commonly ordered that where there is a claim of ongoing problems from the accident, the client and I often agree to the exam without waiting for a court order. Under this rule, the scope of the exam is limited to the ongoing condition being claimed, and we are permitted to have a witness present and to record the exam.

In practice, this exam is very much like the PIP IME. The examiner gets your medical records, she takes a history, performs a physical examination, and generates a report. The objective of the insurance company and its attorney is the same as in the PIP IME: to establish that your treatment was not reasonable, medically necessary, or accident-related. Sometimes, I allow PIP IMEs to go forward without sending a witness, but with Rule 35 examinations, I always send a witness and make a recording because the examining doctor is likely to testify, either in person or by sworn statement, and I want to make absolutely sure he sticks to the truth and reports only what was said and observed during the exam.

Fortunately, as discussed above, most judges and arbitrators understand that these professional examiners, while also practicing doctors, have great financial motivation to give the opinions sought by the insurance companies. As a result, their opinions are generally given less weight than those of your treating doctors. However, juries are often not as savvy as judges and arbitrators. If a persuasive IME doctor gets in front of a jury, it could do great harm to your case. Often in such cases, I will hire our own expert, in addition to your treating doctors, to reinforce the fact that your injuries are real and that your treatment was in fact reasonable, medically necessary, and accident-related.

Often, even in cases that involve a third-party IME, or CR 35 examination, I am able to resolve the claim through settlement. Where I can't, I make sure there is ammunition to counter the examiner's testimony at trial. But regardless of the outcome, the IME is just another hoop the insurance companies make you jump through before you can bring your claim to a successful conclusion.

CONCLUSION

As you can see, both your insurance company and the other insurance company can force you to do several things before you get paid. Whether it's in regards to your medical bills or your pain and suffering, insurance companies have a right to ask for documentation and other evidence before they can be forced to pay. Having a good lawyer on your side can make this process less mysterious and difficult, but even with a good lawyer, it can still feel frustrating and time-consuming. Some of these insurance company hoops take place while you are still getting treatment, and some take place after you have completed your treatment. The next chapter will discuss the transition from active, accident-related treatment to negotiating a settlement for your claim with the insurance company.

CHAPTER 14

MOVING FROM
TREATMENT TO NEGOTIATION

Negotiation is not a policy. It's a technique.
It's something you use when it's to your advantage, and
something that you don't use when it's not to your advantage.

— John Bolton

In the previous chapters, I dealt primarily with the period before your accident and the period from your accident to the conclusion of your medical treatment. But what happens after you've completed your treatment and you are ready to move on with your claim? In this chapter, I will discuss the transition from treatment to negotiation. When your treatment is still ongoing, it is your attorney's job to protect you from all the background noise so you can focus on getting better. Once your treatment is completed, the primary role of your attorney changes from being a protector to being an advocate. Hopefully, your attorney was preparing and organizing evidence to support your case while you were still receiving treatment. Now is the time to put that evidence to good use.

Often, there is nothing unusual about your claim. The accident was clearly the other person's fault, and you were clearly injured. Your treatment was consistent and reasonable, and your doctors all agree that the injuries were a result of the accident. In such claims, just the threat of litigation is usually enough to get a fair settlement offer from the liability insurance company. I collect all of the evidence supporting your claim, including the police report, photos of the vehicles and the accident scene, witness statements, medical records and bills, and anything else that might be useful. I organize this evidence and provide it to the insurance company along with a demand for settlement with a deadline. The deadline is important. If I don't give the insurance company a time limit, it's likely to take months to respond to our demand.

The demand serves three purposes. It provides the insurance company the information it needs to evaluate your claim properly, it demonstrates that I am an experienced professional who knows what I am doing, and it creates a very real threat of litigation. If the claim does not settle, the insurance company knows that a lawsuit will be filed and it will be forced to defend it. Usually, unless there is some complicating factor, the insurance company will make an offer of settlement within thirty days of our demand. While the opening offer is generally low, it provides a starting point for negotiations. I see about 80 to 85 percent of cases settling without the need to file a lawsuit. But even in the most straightforward claim, sometimes the insurance company refuses to make a reasonable offer for reasons the client and I can never know. In those claims, a lawsuit must be filed.

In other claims, some key piece of evidence must be identified and obtained before I can get the insurance company to make an offer.

Those cases require some extra investigation, but what I discover can often make the difference between no recovery at all and a very large recovery.

THE MISSING VIDEO

Did you know that most commercial busses have video cameras that run all the time? I do. But still, in most bus accidents, the carrier pretends the video doesn't exist. This evidence can be the difference between winning and losing a claim, but if you don't know how to get it, you could be out of luck.

In the case of Melissa Parker, the video made all the difference in the world. Melissa was an elderly woman with a balance disorder. Obviously, she couldn't drive. Fortunately, the town in which she lived had a municipal bus service for people with disabilities. All she had to do was call and tell the bus service where to pick her up and the bus would be there at the designated time. Melissa had a standing written agreement with the bus service that required she be assisted from door to door.

On the occasion in question, the bus pulled up to the designated location, and the driver opened the door. The driver remained in her seat, going through some paperwork, so Melissa began to climb the stairs into the bus. Before she made it to the top, she lost her balance and fell backwards, suffering a severe head injury and a broken arm.

When I took the case, I requested all of the relevant information from the bus company (which also happened to be a division of the local government). It provided me with some paperwork, and with a single camera view of the bus without any sound. Unfortunately, none of what it provided was very helpful. Instead of giving up, I filed a public disclosure request with the local government. After several months of waiting, I received the paperwork that proved the bus company had agreed to a "door-to-door" arrangement, which was very specifically described as an agreement to accompany the passenger onto and off of the bus at every stop. I also received a CD with seven different camera views, including audio. One of these views clearly established that Melissa had waited for the bus driver to assist her, but the driver never made a move to get up. Eventually, frustrated with waiting, Melissa attempted to climb the stairs herself, and still, the driver did not move. When Melissa lost her balance, she cried out, but the driver, still with her seat belt fastened, was unable to help in time, so Melissa fell backwards.

It took more than a year for Melissa to heal from her injuries, and because the bones in her arm failed to fuse properly, she needed surgery to repair her fracture. I prepared a comprehensive demand package as I usually do, but it was the video that made the difference. Once the bus company saw that I had the video, it quickly agreed to mediation, and I was able to negotiate a very nice settlement for Melissa.

THE DENIAL

Sometimes, a defendant flat out denies that she did anything wrong, or even that a collision took place. In the case of Eddie Kim, it was a police car video that saved the day. Eddie's car was having mechanical problems and was legally parked on the side of the road. It was a foggy early morning and Eddie was leaning into the backseat of his parked car to retrieve some tools when the car was violently struck by a moving vehicle. The car that hit him then lost control, crossed the center line of the road, and crashed into a tree. Despite the damage to Eddie's car, the skid marks across the road, and the collision with the tree, the driver denied that she had ever hit Eddie's car.

Eddie sustained a fairly serious injury to his shoulder and ribs, and he had some back pain as well. When I contacted the driver's insurance company to advise it of Eddie's claim, it told me that its insured was denying that she ever hit Eddie's car and that it was going to deny liability. I pointed out the police report and showed it photos of the damage to Eddie's car, but the adjuster insisted that the driver never hit Eddie's car.

Fortunately, in Seattle, all police cars are equipped with cameras. All officers wear microphones so the audio is captured as well as the video. We were able to obtain the video of the investigation from the police. The video was a very entertaining fifteen minutes of multiple police officers questioning the defendant. First, she simply denied hitting Eddie's car. After some questioning, she admitted that her windshield was all fogged up and she couldn't see anything. When the officers asked her how her car ended up hitting a tree, she admitted that she "heard a loud noise," which scared her and caused her to lose control of her vehicle. She still denied hitting Eddie's car. Eventually, she admitted that she hit something, which caused her to lose control and swerve across the street into the tree.

We made a copy of the video along with a transcript of the relevant parts and sent it on to the claims adjuster. After a week, the adjuster called to tell us the insurance company would be accepting liability. After that, it was a simple matter to document Eddie's injuries and treatment and prepare a standard demand for settlement. Ultimately, we were able to get a fair settlement for Eddie.

"BUT I STILL NEED SURGERY"

Charlie Daggett was a passenger in his uncle's car. His uncle was going through an intersection when another driver ran a red light and T-boned his uncle's car. Charlie hurt his neck and back, but his worst injury was to his knee. After a doctor visit and a few months of chiropractic and massage, his neck and back were much better, but the knee was not improving. He began a course of physical therapy for the knee with some improvement, but still the knee was weak and painful.

After several months, Charlie's doctor referred him for an MRI of the knee, which confirmed a small tear to the meniscus. Based on the imaging, the doctor gave Charlie two options. He could do nothing and hope the knee improved with time, or he could have surgery to repair the torn meniscus. The doctor advised Charlie that if the knee did not improve with time, he could return for surgery at any time in the future.

Charlie was reluctant to have surgery if there was a chance the knee would improve with time, but he was anxious to settle his injury claim. Although his medical records suggested the possibility of surgery, the insurance company refused to consider the cost of a future procedure that was merely a possibility. Instead, it wanted to treat Charlie's claim as a simple whiplash claim. Without additional documentation, I would not be able to get a fair settlement for Charlie.

I reached out to Charlie's orthopedist, who told me that he believed surgery would be necessary for any meaningful improvement in Charlie's knee. I had him generate a report that documented the injuries to the knee, the need for surgery, and the connection between the motor vehicle accident and the injury. Finally, I had the doctor itemize all of the expenses involved with the future surgery, including any follow-up treatment and rehabilitation. With the help of this report, I was able to get the insurance company to increase its offer, not only to include the cost of all of the future treatment identified by the doctor, but also a significant amount for the pain and suffering that Charlie would experience in connection with the surgery.

To date, Charlie still has not had surgery on his knee. It has improved, but he still experiences weakness and pain on a regular basis. He may never decide to have surgery, but if he does, he will know that his settlement included that cost as well as the pain and down time that would come with it.

DOCTOR NO

While Charlie's doctor was extremely helpful and instrumental in getting a fair settlement from the insurance company, not all doctors are that supportive of their patients' legal claims. The lack of support by a treating doctor can destroy an otherwise good claim.

Ellie Blue was driving through the Battery Street Tunnel in Seattle when traffic ahead of her suddenly stopped. Ellie was able to stop in time, but the following driver was distracted by her two children in the backseat and never even attempted to slow down. She rear-ended Ellie's compact car at high speed. Both drivers pulled off the road, and the police came and made a report. Ellie was transported by ambulance to the hospital.

Ellie had no problems with her neck or back before this accident, and she had no history of treatment for any neck or back-related issues. Following the collision, Ellie's care was managed by her primary care doctor at Virginia Mason Medical Center. At first, she was treated for strains to her neck and back, but when the symptoms continued to worsen, her doctor referred Ellie to a physiatrist, a specialist in physical medicine and rehabilitation. This doctor encouraged Ellie to continue the chiropractic, massage, and acupuncture treatments she was receiving. He also ordered diagnostic testing, which was positive for some bulging discs in the neck, but not enough to warrant surgery. He ordered a series of nerve block injections in Ellie's neck, but still the symptoms persisted.

As the three-year deadline to file a lawsuit approached, I prepared a demand package to send to the insurance company. Although Ellie's injuries had not resolved, they were severe enough, and her treatment extensive enough, that we felt confident we would be able to get the insurance policy limits. In preparing her demand, I reached out to the physiatrist. This doctor had followed Ellie's condition for over two years, and he had ordered or referred most of the testing and treatment that Ellie had undergone. The doctor refused to state that the injuries he was treating and the treatment he prescribed were related to the motor vehicle accident. Even worse, he wouldn't even state that the treatment he ordered was reasonable or medically necessary. His reasoning was that because there was no objective reason he could determine for the ongoing pain and disability in Ellie's neck, he was unable to give an opinion as to the cause. With respect to the reasonableness, he stated that he had an obligation to believe his patients and treat the symptoms they present with, but he would not say the treatment was reasonable.

Imagine my position when I had to call my client and explain to her that her trusted doctor—the doctor she had cried to for the past two years—had just sabotaged her claim. Without his testimony, there was no way we could go to trial. Upon filing a lawsuit, one of the first things the defense attorney would do is take the deposition of Ellie's treating doctor. After that, she might not get anything. She couldn't believe it. All she had done was tell her doctor what she was experiencing and followed his recommendations. There was no other explanation for the neck pain. Despite this setback, we had to push for the best settlement we could get. Even with an outside expert witness testifying that the treatment was reasonable and medically necessary, the testimony of Ellie's own treating doctor would be too damaging to overcome.

In the end, I got a decent settlement for Ellie, but I am certain I should have gotten her more, and I would have if her doctor had been willing to defend his own treatment and the treatment and testing that he ordered. I often advise my clients not to discuss their legal situations with their doctors. In general, doctors don't want to be involved in the legal process. They want to treat their patients and practice medicine. However, in certain cases, it is useful to make sure the doctor agrees that the injuries he is treating are related to the accident. If he doesn't, and your treatment might be an issue in the case, you may want to find a different doctor.

SELF-EMPLOYED LOST INCOME

An uncooperative doctor isn't the only thing that can make a case difficult to settle. When my 2002 car accident happened, my law practice was still in its early stages but growing rapidly. I did not have any employees, and I did everything myself. I did all the marketing and management. I answered the phones, I did the books, and I prepared the taxes. And, of course, I did all the legal work. Over the first few months following my accident, I missed several days from work, and even when I was working, I was distracted and limited in what I could do. I was able to take care of all of my clients, but without question, I would have earned more money had it not been for the accident.

The problem was I did not have regular hours or a regular salary. When a typical employee misses work following an accident, I just get documentation from his workplace showing his rate of pay and how much work he missed and submit it to the insurance company for reimbursement. With a self-employed person, it can be more difficult. Usually, I will get the business books or tax filings for the prior years to show how much income was earned per week or per month before the accident and compare it to income earned after the accident, but with a growing business, this method does not work either. The fact is that, although I earned more in the year following my accident than I did in the previous year, I would have earned even more had it not been for the injuries.

Lost income for a self-employed person in a growing business is one of the most difficult elements of damage to prove. Ultimately, I settled my claim for an amount that included the equivalent of two weeks of lost income. While I'm sure my actual lost income was more, even I was unable to calculate it with any degree of certainty, and this settlement was probably the best I could hope to get. (And yes, I did have an attorney dealing with the insurance company on my behalf. I'm no fool.)

CONCLUSION

As you can see, you and your lawyers need to take many steps before you begin negotiations to maximize your recovery. Documenting your medical bills, lost wages, and other expenses is the easy part. In the next chapter, I will discuss how to maximize your recovery for your non-economic damages—your pain and suffering.

CHAPTER 15

VALUING YOUR PAIN AND SUFFERING

At a certain level of suffering or injustice no one can do anything for anyone. Pain is solitary.

— Albert Camus

In the previous chapter, I discussed transitioning your claim from treatment into the negotiation phase, and the kinds of factors that can either strengthen or weaken your claim. In this chapter, I will discuss the most intangible and difficult to prove element of damages in your claim. This element of non-economic or "general" damages is most commonly referred to as "pain and suffering," but it is so much more. It includes physical pain and emotional pain, both in the past and future. It includes disability, disfigurement, and loss of enjoyment of life. It includes fear, frustration, worry, doubt, uncertainty, and sadness. The law provides no formula for placing a dollar value on any of these "intangibles," and so it is ultimately up to a jury to determine what they are worth. If you want to settle your claim, you and the insurance company will have to agree on the value of your pain and suffering. In order to maximize your claim, a good attorney will get to know you and how your injuries have affected your life. He will then make sure the insurance company knows exactly how your life has been turned upside-down, and he will seek to get you a recovery for each type of non-economic damage recognized by the law.

PHYSICAL PAIN AND MENTAL ANGUISH

The most common element of non-economic damages, present in pretty much every case I see, is a claim for physical pain and mental anguish. This is the actual pain a person suffers from his injury and the direct emotional impact it has on the person's life. This element is truly "pain and suffering," although it is only a portion of the non-economic damages an injured person may recover.

In presenting a claim for pain and suffering, either in a demand to an insurance company, to an arbitrator, or to a jury, it is essential that the pain and the resulting emotional distress be described with as much specificity as possible. For example, which of the following descriptions gives you a clearer picture of a person's pain? "When I tilt my head back, I get a headache," or "I have a dull throbbing at the base of my skull all the time, and when I tilt my head back, I get a sharp stabbing pain like someone is driving a nail through my left temple and into my brain."

Pain can be burning, stabbing, aching, pulsing, throbbing, sharp, electric, constant, or intermittent. It can be all over or in a very specific part of your body. It can be there all the time, or only when you do certain things. If you are able to describe the pain with as much detail as possible, it will help your attorney present your case more effectively. If your attorney is not asking you these questions, perhaps you should bring it up with her.

When I was injured, I first felt tightness and burning on the right side of my neck and below my right shoulder blade. After a few months, as those symptoms improved, I began to notice a deep aching in my left lower back and hip. Eventually, this ache progressed to a sharp, shooting pain from my lower back, through my hip, and down my left leg all the way to my two little toes. Being able to describe the pain this way helped my doctors diagnose and treat my condition, but it also helped support my legal claim for damages.

In addition to the actual pain from the injury, there is the emotional suffering that goes along with it. This suffering can be in the form of despair or hopelessness, fear, anxiety, frustration, anger, depression, and more. In a typical case, emotional distress can be established without the need for mental health treatment, but in the most severe cases, an injured person needs to seek counseling for depression or anxiety.

In my case, I was afraid I would never get back to my pre-accident condition, that I would always be in pain, and that I would always be limited in what I could do. I worried I wouldn't be as good a provider for my family and that I wouldn't be as fun to be around. I worried that I would always have to go to doctor appointments and that my injuries would dominate my life. While most of those worries turned out to be unfounded, they were real, and the law provides compensation for them.

I have seen many cases where my client was terrified to get into a car for weeks or even months following an accident. In cases like these, a behavioral therapist can help him overcome his fears while at the same time providing documentation to support the claim for emotional distress.

DISABILITY, DISFIGUREMENT, AND LOSS OF ENJOYMENT OF LIFE

As discussed above, what people often refer to as "pain and suffering" actually includes much more. The law does not define disability, but courts have interpreted it to mean not only the inability to work, but also the impairment of a person's ability to lead a normal life. Loss of enjoyment of life differs from disability where it involves the loss of a specific unusual activity, such as ballet dancing or playing the violin. Cosmetic disfigurement is a separate item because of the mental suffering that may accompany it.

I have had clients with claims that involve all of these components of pain and suffering.

First, as with physical pain, virtually every case involves some degree of disability. Because disability simply means the inability to lead a normal life, it includes things like not being able to make your bed or go shopping for groceries. Even being unable to work out in the gym counts as a disability if that was part of your pre-injury routine. It is important in every case to catalogue what kinds of activities you are unable to do or are limited in doing after the accident that you were previously able to do without limitation.

Loss of enjoyment of life is more specific, and I have seen it as an issue with musicians, bodybuilders, and yoga instructors, to name a few. Jennifer Shaw was a violinist who injured her lower back and neck in a rear-end accident. Prior to the accident, she would practice playing her violin for several hours each day, but after the accident, she couldn't sit with her violin for more than ten minutes without severely aggravating her pain. In this case, her inability to play the violin was an additional element of damages, separate from her ordinary pain and suffering or disability. Had she been unable to resume playing the violin as her injuries healed, she would have been entitled to recover for future loss of enjoyment of life, as well as the future lost income she might suffer from not being able to play.

Finally, disfigurement pretty much speaks for itself. For instance, a scar or other visible mark that changes a person's visible appearance. The bigger the disfigurement, the more it can be worth. Also, the amount of compensation you receive could be affected by the scar's location. A three-inch scar on a person's face is worth more than a three-inch scar on her leg.

Julie Boyd was visiting a friend when she was attacked by the friend's large dog. The attack resulted in a dislocated shoulder and a deep scar from her nose across her lip to her chin. I had Julie evaluated by an excellent, local plastic surgeon, who had experience testifying at trial. The surgeon recommended a course of treatment to reduce the appearance of the scar, but he stated that even after the procedure, the scar would still be visible. I was able to use that report to get a substantial recovery for Julie.

DAMAGES FOR INJURIES TO A LOVED ONE

Even if you weren't the one injured, you may still be entitled to a recovery for non-economic damages resulting from the injury to a spouse or parent. Historically, loss of consortium claims were derived from the husband's presumed property right to the "services" of his wife. Although the claim included the wife's contributions to the household, it was generally understood to be a loss of sex when the wife suffered an injury.

In modern times, the loss of consortium claim has been extended to the impact an injury has on the relationship between spouses, or between a parent and a child. It includes emotional support, love, attention, care, services, companionship, and assistance. As a person who has been injured, but who has also been the spouse of an injured person, I can tell you that it's sometimes just as hard to be the spouse. While the injured partner is suffering both physically and emotionally, the uninjured spouse has to take up the slack by doing more household chores while at the same time being emotionally supportive. All the while, the injured spouse has little energy to give the emotional support required by any relationship, and the relationship can be strained or even broken. I have seen several relationships end because the uninjured partner could not tolerate being with the injured person any longer. We often suggest some kind of couples counseling in situations like this, but sometimes, the impact on the relationship is too great to be repaired.

In the case of an injured parent, a child may have a claim for loss of love, care, companionship, and guidance. This claim is separate from a claim a child might have for the wrongful death of a parent.

CONCLUSION

As you can see, what we commonly refer to as "pain and suffering" actually includes more. It can include physical pain, mental anguish, disability, disfigurement, and loss of enjoyment of life. If you have been injured in an accident, take a moment to consider what elements of non-economic damages you have suffered, write them in the lines below, and make sure to share them with your attorney. You should include a description of your pain, as well as any activities that have been limited or otherwise affected by your injuries. I find it sometimes helps to divide the effects into broad categories such as home, work, and social, and then to get as specific as possible within each category. Ultimately, the more detail you can provide about how your injuries affected your life, the better chance your attorney has to maximize your recovery from the insurance company.

_____

_____

_____

_____

_____

_____

_____

CHAPTER 16

FILING A LAWSUIT—
TO SUE OR NOT TO SUE

Every lawsuit results from somebody doing something wrong.
If everybody did right, we wouldn't need laws.

— Alan Dershowitz

In the last chapter, we discussed your non-economic damages—what they are and how to maximize your recovery for them. Ideally, those damages are bundled with your money damages or "special damages" in a demand package, and after negotiations with the insurance company, you are able to negotiate a fair settlement. Most of the time, if your claim is good, a negotiated settlement can provide the best opportunity to compensate you for your injuries. Of course, money never makes what happened to you okay, but for the most part, it's all the law has to offer, and it certainly can help. Sometimes, however, the insurance company refuses to make a fair offer to settle your claim. In those cases, we have little choice but to file a lawsuit. In this chapter, I will discuss how a lawsuit gets filed, and we will explore the risks and benefits of taking your case toward trial.

SUMMONS AND COMPLAINT

The act of starting a lawsuit in Washington is really quite simple. You need a Summons and a Complaint. Depending on the court you are filing in, you can start the lawsuit by either filing the papers with the court or having the papers served on the defendant. Whichever one you do first, you will ultimately need to do the other as well.

A Summons is a legal document that notifies the defendant that he or she is being sued, and it instructs the person on how to respond to the lawsuit. This is a generic form and does not contain any facts about the particular claim. In Washington, as in most states, you are not allowed to sue the insurance company. Instead, the actual defendant must be served. If he has insurance, he will probably just forward the papers to his insurance company, which will hire a lawyer to prepare a response. Lawyers usually forward a copy to the insurance company themselves just so the insurance company knows a lawsuit has been started and that the insurance company has a limited amount of time to reply.

While the Summons gives notice that a lawsuit is being started, the Complaint sets forth what the claim is about. Washington is a notice pleading state, which means the Complaint need only state the barest facts necessary to let the defendant know what he is being sued for and what is the remedy sought. I remember a multiple choice question on the bar exam asking which of the following was a valid Complaint. The correct answer was: "He stole my skateboard. I want it back." This answer identifies a defendant (he), alleges what he did wrong (stole my skateboard), and proposes a remedy (I want it back).

In a typical auto case, the Complaint is a bit more comprehensive, but not by much. It states who the parties are, where they reside, and where the incident took place in order to establish jurisdiction of the court. It states what the defendant did; in most cases, he failed to exercise reasonable care in the operation of his vehicle resulting in injuries to the plaintiff. Finally, a remedy is sought. In negligence cases in Washington, a specific amount of damages is not set forth in the Complaint. Rather, an amount of money is asked for that will compensate the plaintiff for her damages, both past and future.

Once the Summons and Complaint have been filed and served, the lawsuit is officially underway. In King County Superior Court, the entire pre-trial calendar is set immediately upon filing. This contains deadlines for all kinds of events that take place before trial. In other jurisdictions, the calendar is more flexible. In every jurisdiction, though, the filing of the lawsuit is just the beginning of what can be a long and difficult road to trial. In the next chapter, I will discuss the slow pace of the court system, but in this chapter, I will continue to explore the pros and cons of filing a lawsuit and the limitations of trial.

THE JURY

When I was a new attorney working in a small Seattle firm, the firm represented a woman in a very sad claim. Brenda Johnson was a minority woman receiving public assistance, and she was pregnant with twins. At some point in the pregnancy, she began to notice cramping and an unusual discharge. She called her doctor, who advised her to come in for her next regularly scheduled appointment in a week. Two days later, Brenda called in again, deeply concerned. The doctor had her come in, but he did not perform an ultrasound and sent her home without any resolution to the problem. Four days later, Brenda returned to the emergency room in premature labor. When an ultrasound was performed, the problem was finally detected.

Brenda was suffering from a condition called twin-twin transfusion syndrome. This condition results when the blood vessels in the placenta favor one twin over the other, resulting in a shortage of blood for one twin and too much for the other. This condition is detectable by ultrasound and can be treated in utero. In Brenda's case, had the ultrasound been performed in a timely manner, the condition would have been identified, and she would have been admitted to the hospital. Even if the premature delivery couldn't have been avoided, the hospital staff would have been able to administer steroids to accelerate the babies' lung development. Sadly, in Brenda's case, by the time the problem was discovered, it was too late to do anything. The smaller twin was stillborn, and the larger twin was born prematurely, with underdeveloped lungs, and suffered profound brain damage. She will spend the rest of her life in a wheelchair with severe mental and physical disabilities.

My boss consulted with, and ultimately hired, some of the top experts on twin-twin transfusion in the country. Because the primary plaintiff was the surviving child, the court appointed an independent attorney called a *guardian ad litem* to be involved in the process and to make sure everything was done in the child's best interest. When we were unable to negotiate a fair settlement, a lawsuit was filed and we prepared for trial. After months of depositions, pretrial motions, and negotiations, we found ourselves at trial. It should be noted that, at this point, the defendant hospital had made an offer of $3 million to settle the claims. I had only been practicing law for a year, so I really had no basis to evaluate this offer, but based on the expected testimony of our expert witnesses and jury verdicts for similar injuries around the country, my employer and the *guardian ad litem* agreed that the case was worth more.

The first day of trial was a whirlwind of activity. First was a final round of pretrial motions and discussions regarding how the judge would instruct the jury regarding the case and how the jury members were to make their decision. After lunch, jury selection began. One by one, potential jurors were eliminated, and by the end of the day, the final jury panel was complete. On the way out of the courtroom that afternoon, the attorney for the hospital approached my boss and invited him to resume settlement negotiations, indicating there was more money that could be made available. I don't know

FILING A LAWSUIT—TO SUE OR NOT TO SUE

whether the hospital intended to increase its offer by half a million or a million or more, and nobody will ever know because my boss advised the attorney that the time for negotiation had passed, and that he intended to win at trial.

Trial continued for more than a week, and after all of the heartbreaking evidence, the jury was sent to deliberate. The defense had argued that the hospital didn't do anything wrong, and that even if the condition had been detected earlier, nothing could have been done about it. Our experts obviously testified that the condition would have been detected and could have been remedied had the hospital only done what the minimum standard of care requires in a high-risk pregnancy and performed the ultrasound.

During their deliberations, the jury members sent several written questions to the judge that indicated their thought processes. One question asked what would happen to the doctors involved if they found against the hospital. Another had to do with other causes of birth defects besides twin-twin transfusion. It should be noted that no argument was ever made that the twin-twin transfusion was not the cause of the brain damage suffered by the surviving child. After three days of deliberations, the jury came back with a verdict in favor of the defense.

At the end of the trial, several of the jurors approached us to report what they rightfully considered to be misconduct by other jurors. Apparently, one of the jurors had contacted a lawyer he knew to discuss legal aspects of the case and shared what he learned with the rest of the jurors. Another juror did independent research on the Internet regarding other possible causes of birth defects and shared his findings with the jury as well. We obtained sworn statements from the complaining jurors and presented them to the judge, asking for a mistrial. The judge denied our motion and the appeal was denied. Case closed.

I learned some valuable lessons from this experience, and you can learn them as well. First, sometimes there is no choice but to file a lawsuit. When the case has a high value and the insurance company is not willing to engage in meaningful negotiations, a lawsuit is your only remaining option. You need to consider when entering into a lawsuit that the process leading to trial is long, expensive, and difficult, but in certain cases, it is your best option. Second, never stop negotiating. Sitting down at the negotiating table does not force you to accept the defendant's offer, but at least you will know what you are turning down. Even now, years after the fact, when I imagine the life that poor child could have had if the case had settled, I am heartbroken. It may have been the right choice to turn down the hospital's offer and continue to try the case, but I will always believe we should have heard out the other side. The third and perhaps most important lesson is that juries are unpredictable. Jurors may have a bias. They may bring in outside information. They may not believe your key witness. There is absolutely no such thing as a sure thing when it comes to a jury trial. If you decide to take your case to trial, and sometimes you must, you'd better make sure it's a strong case, well-prepared, and well-executed, just to give yourself a chance at a fair recovery.

HOT COFFEE

I previously mentioned the possibility of juror bias, and I can't mention that topic without talking about the McDonald's hot coffee case. Most people think they know all the facts of that case, and most of them are dead wrong. The big takeaway from the McDonald's case is not the facts of the case, but how the case has been used since then, and the public perception around it. Still, a summary of the facts is in order. Before you read this section, review what you think you know about the case. Then see how many important facts you had wrong and ask whether it changes your opinion of the case.

In February, 1992, Stella Liebeck, a seventy-nine-year-old woman from Albuquerque, New Mexico, ordered a cup of coffee from the drive-thru window of a local McDonald's restaurant. Ms. Liebeck was not the driver of the car, but the passenger of her grandson Chris, who was driving. Chris parked the car so Ms. Liebeck could add cream and sugar to her coffee. She placed the cup between her legs and pulled the far side of the lid toward her. As she was removing the lid, the cup tipped toward her and spilled onto her lap. Liebeck was wearing cotton sweatpants, which absorbed the coffee and held it against her skin, resulting in third-degree burns on 6 percent of her skin, including her thighs, buttocks, and groin, and lesser burns over 16 percent of her skin. Ms. Liebeck spent eight days in the hospital where she underwent skin grafting for the burns. During that time, she lost twenty pounds, reducing her weight to eighty-six pounds. She suffered significant permanent scarring, and was partially disabled for nearly two years following the incident.

Ms. Liebeck's medical bills were $10,500, and she anticipated future medical bills of $2,500. In addition to her medical bills, her daughter suffered a loss of income of $5,000 while caring for her mother. Ms. Liebeck tried to settle the claim herself, asking for $20,000. McDonald's responded by offering $800. At that point, feeling she had no other choice, Liebeck hired an attorney who filed a lawsuit in New Mexico District Court. After the lawsuit was filed, Ms. Liebeck's attorney offered to settle for $90,000 and McDonald's again refused. Just before trial, Ms. Liebeck again offered to settle for $300,000. A mediator suggested $225,000, but McDonald's again refused.

At trial, Ms. Liebeck's attorney presented evidence that McDonald's required its franchises to hold coffee at 180-190 degrees. At 190 degrees, coffee will cause a third-degree burn in two to seven seconds. Documents obtained from McDonald's during pre-trial discovery showed that in the ten years prior to this incident, more than 700 people had been burned by McDonald's coffee; many of these claims had been quietly settled by McDonald's.

After hearing all of the evidence from Ms. Liebeck and from McDonald's and deliberating, a twelve-person jury found that Mc-

Donalds was 80 percent responsible for the incident and that Ms. Liebeck was 20 percent liable. It awarded Ms. Liebeck $200,000 in compensatory damages to cover her medical bills, lost income, and her non-economic damages (see Chapter 18). It then reduced this amount by 20 percent to $160,000. In addition, it awarded $2.7 million in punitive damages to punish McDonald's for its willful disregard for its customers' safety. This figure was based on two days' worth of coffee revenues earned by the company. It should be noted that the State of Washington does not allow a recovery for punitive damages except in very narrowly defined cases. In Washington, Ms. Liebeck's total recovery would have been $160,000. The judge immediately reduced the punitive damage award to $480,000 for a total award of $640,000. The decision was appealed by both Ms. Liebeck and McDonald's, and the case was ultimately settled out of court for less than $600,000.

Did you know all of that? If you did, you are one of very few people who do. Now, you can agree or disagree with the outcome of this case, but if you ask me, $600,000 for the kind of injuries suffered by Ms. Liebeck doesn't even come close to compensating her for what she went through.

As I said at the outset, what is most important about the McDonald's case is not its specific facts, but how it has been used by the insurance industry and big business to stir up hostility against the civil justice system generally and against injured people and their lawyers more specifically. This case has been the centerpiece of a sustained and concerted effort to persuade people that civil lawsuits are bad, that juries are out of control, that trial lawyers are greedy and self-interested, and that strict limits should be placed on damage awards and on attorney fees to prevent this from happening again. The insurance industry and big business interests have been waging a campaign to persuade people that compensating people for injuries suffered as a result of someone else's negligence is bad for America and bad for each person. It argues that large damage awards result in higher insurance premiums, and it encourages skepticism toward anyone who makes a claim for damages. For more information on the McDonald's case and how it has been used to dismantle the protections of the civil justice system, I highly recommend the documentary *Hot Coffee*.

In fact, statistics regarding lawsuits in the United States clearly demonstrate that there is no frivolous lawsuit problem. The Rand Institute for Civil Justice, one of the most respected think tanks in the country, found that only 10 percent of injured people seek compensation and only 2 percent of them file lawsuits. It found that since 1991, personal injury claims accounted for less than 6 percent of all cases filed. Other reports have shown that while populations have grown across the country, personal injury lawsuits have decreased by 21 percent. The frivolous lawsuit myth is an invention of insurance companies and big business.

I could write a whole book about the lies underlying the tort reform movement, the ongoing effort by some special interests to dismantle the protections of the civil justice system, but that really isn't my point here. My point is that when you're deciding whether to settle or go to trial, you should think about who might be on the jury and how he or she has been influenced. Do the jurors know the facts of the McDonald's case? Have they been persuaded that there's an epidemic of "frivolous lawsuits"? Do they fear that giving you a fair recovery will raise their own insurance rates? Will they assume you are greedy just for seeking fair compensation? These are real concerns and must be considered in every case that goes to trial.

"WE LIKED THE CLIENT BUT NOT THE DOCTOR"

Sometimes, the jury likes a plaintiff and wants to give her an award, but it either doesn't like one of her doctors, doesn't understand the process, or a little bit of both. Several years ago, I represented Mariella Phillips in an auto claim. Mariella was driving through a parking lot when another driver backed out of a parking space and T-boned Mariella's vehicle, throwing her head and body from side to side. She was hurt, and after being checked out at the emergency room, she missed a week of work and underwent nearly six months of chiropractic and massage treatment. Between her medical bills and lost income, Mariella had about $10,000 in economic damages.

After unsuccessfully attempting to settle the claim, I filed a lawsuit and proceeded to arbitration, where Mariella was awarded $27,000. The insurance company immediately appealed the arbitration award and forced us to retry the case to a jury. At trial, the defendant admitted fault for the accident, but the insurance company lawyer questioned the medical treatment and bills. I called the chiropractor as a witness to explain the injuries he had found and the treatment he had provided. Although he was a bit nervous on the stand, I thought his testimony was adequate to show that the injuries were real and related to the accident and that the treatment he provided was reasonable.

The trial took two days, and after a couple of hours of deliberating, the jury returned with a verdict of $12,000, including $10,000 for Mariella's medical bills and lost income and $2,000 for her pain and suffering. When I interviewed the jurors after the case, they said they liked our client and believed she was hurt in the accident, but they did not like the chiropractor. They felt he had tricked her into getting more treatment than she needed, even though she testified that she was in real pain and the treatment helped her recover. Some of them genuinely thought they were being generous by awarding all of her bills and an additional $2,000 for pain and suffering. Maybe they didn't know that the attorney gets paid a percentage of the recovery, or that it can cost thousands of dollars to try a case. Maybe they didn't care. Either way, the award wasn't enough to pay all the bills, let alone compensate Mariella for having to endure her injuries.

I was able to negotiate a reduction in the doctor's bills, but it still wasn't enough.

When you are considering whether to take your case to trial, you need to think about how a jury of strangers might value your injuries. What will they think of your treatment choices? Will they like and believe your doctors? What value will they place on your pain and suffering? These are all questions you must consider before abandoning settlement efforts and taking your chances at trial.

MAKING THEM PAY

Of course, sometimes a jury goes the other way. In Washington, either party can require arbitration in cases where the damages are less than $50,000. I will discuss arbitration as a possible alternative to trial in Chapter 19. The advantage of this kind of arbitration is that it is quicker and less expensive than trial. One of the disadvantages is that it's non-binding. That means even if you win the arbitration, the insurance company can appeal and force you to present your case to a jury. However, there is risk to the insurance company in appealing the arbitration award. If it fails to improve its position at trial, it has to pay not only the jury verdict, but your attorney fees as well.

Paul Jackson was stopped at a red light when he was rear-ended by another vehicle. The driver of the following car was speaking on her cell phone and never even tried to slow down. Paul's car was totaled, and when all was said and done, he had nearly $15,000 in medical bills, including ambulance, emergency room, primary care physician, chiropractic, and massage therapy. After the insurance company refused to offer more than Paul's medical bills, I filed a lawsuit and proceeded to arbitration. I presented all of the evidence supporting Paul's claim in a half-day hearing, and the arbitrator awarded Paul $38,000. Although I had asked for more, Paul and I thought this was a fair outcome, and we were prepared to accept it. The insurance company had other ideas.

Shortly after receiving the arbitrator's decision, the insurance company attorney filed a request for trial de novo, which is basically a new trial, and demanded a twelve-person jury. We had already conducted all of the discovery we needed, so we spent the next six months preparing for trial. We discussed the case in great detail with Paul's doctors, and spent several days with Paul and his family preparing them for trial.

After a two-day trial, at which Paul, his wife, and his chiropractor testified, the jury took less than an hour to award him $60,000. In discussing the case with several of the jurors, it was clear they did not like the defendant, who they felt was indifferent to the harm she had caused Paul. They were especially responsive to Paul's wife, who had cried on the stand as she described the impact Paul's injuries had on their relationship, and on his interaction with their two small children.

Clearly, in this case, the insurance company failed to improve its position by appealing the arbitrator's award. In fact, the trial resulted in a far worse result for the insurance company. As a result of the jury's award, the insurance company had to pay not only the $60,000 awarded, but nearly $20,000 in additional attorney fees and costs.

A TREE FALLS IN GEORGIA

Sometimes, the injuries are so catastrophic, and the position of the defendant is so unreasonable, that there is absolutely no choice but to go to trial. In 2010, Shanta Greene was riding as a passenger in a car through a residential area of Savannah, Georgia, when a tree branch fell into the car, impaling her. She lost her right leg and pelvis, suffered brain damage, and is now permanently confined to a wheelchair. Fortunately, she was represented by my good friend Howard Spiva.

Howard argued that the City of Savannah had a basic duty to maintain its trees and make sure they didn't create an unreasonable hazard for drivers and pedestrians. The City refused to negotiate. In a nine-day trial, Howard introduced evidence that the City's Park and Tree Department should have known this particular tree created a hazard because it had dropped a limb three years earlier. He argued that such knowledge put the City on notice and required it to remove the tree or at least to take some kind of corrective action.

After a day of deliberations, a jury awarded Ms. Greene $12 million. The City appealed the jury verdict, but ultimately, it agreed to settle the claim for $9.5 million.

CONCLUSION

The decision of whether or not to go to trial can be a difficult one. Once a lawsuit is filed, the expenses of the claim begin to add up. These expenses can include filing fees, legal messengers, court reporters, expert witnesses, travel, and more. After filing, the burden on the plaintiff increases as well. There are intrusive questions and investigations into your life. There are long delays at a time when you and your family need the money. There is significant risk that for one reason or another, a jury might give you less than what your claim is worth, or even nothing at all. That being said, sometimes filing a lawsuit is obviously the best, if not the only option. In a case like Paul Jackson's, where the insurance company appeals an arbitration award, or like Shanta Greene's, where the defendant adamantly denies liability and the injuries are catastrophic, there is no option but to take the defendant to court and have a jury force it to take responsibility for its negligence. In the next chapter, we will discuss what happens in the months (and sometimes years) after you've made the decision to file a lawsuit.

CHAPTER 17

ENDURING THE SLOW PACE OF JUSTICE

Wheels of justice grind slow but grind fine.

— Sun Tzu

In the previous chapter, I discussed the decision whether to file a lawsuit and factors that may affect that decision. In this chapter, I address what happens after you file a lawsuit. You might have the impression from movies and TV that you file a lawsuit and then get to the courtroom within a few weeks or months. Sadly, that is far from true. In King County, a civil lawsuit is assigned a trial date more than eighteen months from the date of filing. Even then, the trial is often pushed to a later date due to requests of one of the parties or unavailability of a judge. The slow pace of the pretrial process can be frustrating—especially when you need the money—but it also provides you and your attorney a valuable opportunity to prepare your case for the strongest possible presentation at trial. A good attorney will use this time wisely, planning strategy, lining up witnesses, and preparing exhibits and pretrial motions to give you the best possible chance of winning at trial.

After you file a lawsuit, there are often long periods of downtime followed by flurries of activity. Even though you may feel like nothing is happening with your case during the down periods, a good lawyer will be using this time to prepare your case and to be ready for the inevitable activity that's just down the road. There are interrogatories (written questions) and records requests, witness interviews and depositions. There are pre-trial motions, negotiations, and mediations. Many things have to happen between filing and actually getting into the courtroom.

EAT SLOWLY—CHEW YOUR FOOD

My grandfather, William Richman, was a lawyer in New York City. His certificate of admission to the New York Bar in 1930 hangs in my office. He had a small office and spent most of his career as a general practitioner, taking on whatever jobs came his way. It didn't make him rich, but he was able to provide for his family. I never got to know him well. He died suddenly when I was ten years old from a massive heart attack. I never got to ask him about his career as a lawyer, his service as an Air Force officer during World War II, or really anything of substance.

I already shared about the dandelion story, where he would send me and my sister to pick dandelions in order to get us outside playing and let the adults handle adult issues. Another fond memory I have of my grandfather is a saying he would repeat every time we sat down to eat a meal: "Eat slowly. Chew your food." He said it so many times it became a joke for us. My sister and I would repeat it back and forth to each other: "Eat slowly. Chew your food." Even now, when I speak to my wife about my grandfather, she knows that one of the first things I'll say is "Eat slowly. Chew your food." Now I say it to my son, although not at every meal.

As a child, I never really thought about why my grandfather gave us this advice, which seemed so wise and mysterious. But as an adult and a parent, I think about it all the time. Sitting down with your meal is a great opportunity to take a break from the busyness of the day. By having a ritual, whether saying some kind of blessing or even saying, "Eat slowly. Chew your food," the mealtime is somehow separated from the rest of your day. It becomes a special time dedicated to eating a meal and connecting as a family. Also, the act of eating slowly and chewing your food is simply a healthy choice. When you eat slowly, your body can register that you've eaten and will feel full before you finish, resulting in less overeating. When you chew your food, you prevent choking and give your body an opportunity to digest it fully, and you receive the maximum nutritional benefit from what you are eating.

Likewise, although pretrial preparation can seem excruciatingly slow, it is important that you and your lawyer eat slowly and chew your food in preparing your case. By "eating slowly," your lawyer applies a process to preparing your case. Instead of randomly discovering facts and chasing witnesses, your lawyer pauses to assess the strengths and weaknesses of your claim, develop strategies and legal arguments, and determine what evidence he needs to support those arguments. It is a pause to separate the planning and preparation of your claim from the busyness of a typical law practice. By "chewing his food," your lawyer takes each task one at a time and sticks with it until it is completely and thoroughly done in exactly the best way to support your claim. Whether it is interviewing a witness, preparing a legal brief in support of a pretrial motion, or anticipating the instructions a judge will give to the jury in your case, it is essential that your lawyer "eat slowly and chew his food." Not only will this slow preparation maximize your chances of getting a full recovery for your injuries, but it will also minimize the risk of choking—in this case, dropping the ball or missing a key piece of evidence or legal argument.

As a lawyer, I understand your frustration with waiting for months to have your day in court, but I assure you that time is not wasted. If you have the right lawyer, you can use this delay to your advantage.

ROUTINE DELAY

The fact is that delay is built into the system. In King County, when you file a lawsuit, you are given a "Case Scheduling Order." This order is basically a schedule of the events and deadlines that will come up before your case gets to trial. The first event on this schedule is nearly six months after filing. During these six months, the attorneys are expected to conduct discovery (I will discuss the discovery process in the next chapter), and investigate the case. Three months after that, the parties are required to disclose the witnesses they are likely to call at trial. This is only a preliminary list, and it may be supplemented as new witnesses are discovered or additional testimony becomes necessary.

The discovery period stays open for nearly a year after filing. The reality is that during this period, there are long lulls when nothing really happens. Hopefully, your lawyer is continuing to prepare your case for trial, but from the client's point of view, it can seem like nothing is happening for months at a time. After the close of discovery (which is often extended by the judge), things finally start to speed up. The parties are required to participate in some kind of alternative dispute resolution process such as mediation, and if the case does not settle, the parties are required to exchange final lists of the witnesses and exhibits they will use at trial.

After the exchange of witness and exhibit lists comes the deadline for motions that can partially or fully resolve the case in favor of one side. These are also called *motions for summary judgment* or *motions to dismiss*. A partial summary judgment motion will resolve one issue, leaving the rest to be determined at trial. A motion to dismiss or motion for summary judgment will completely resolve the case in favor of one party or the other, making the trial unnecessary.

After the dispositive motions, if the case has not been resolved, a flurry of activity occurs in the weeks leading up to trial. Trial briefs and proposed jury instructions are submitted to the judge, and final arrangements are made for scheduling of witnesses. Finally, the day of trial arrives, and you get to present your case to a jury.

This pre-trial period can be excruciatingly slow for a person who has been injured and wants justice and compensation. Maybe you've fallen behind on paying your bills. Maybe your family and other personal relationships have been affected. Maybe you've lost your job. Certainly, your life has been changed in ways you never expected, and probably not for the better. You want to tell your story, and you want the defendant to pay. During the long period of discovery, it can feel like you've been forgotten and nothing is happening with your case.

We encourage our clients to reach out to us during the pretrial period with any questions or concerns they may have. We also make a commitment to every client that we will communicate with him or her at least once a month to give an update on the process—even if nothing has happened. The reality is that the wheels of justice truly turn slowly, but a good lawyer will guide you through that process with patience and encouragement, while using the opportunity the time allows to prepare your case fully to be presented to a jury.

"WHAT HAPPENED TO MY FACE?"

Sometimes, the delay in getting your case to trial isn't just frustrating; it's downright scary. You are likely heading to trial because you and your lawyer believe your case will have a certain outcome, but the insurance company believes it will have a different outcome. As discussed earlier, jury trials can be unpredictable and many factors, including some completely out of your control, can determine how a jury will rule. All you can do is hire the best professional you can find and trust that you've done everything you can to maximize your chances.

I can understand, on a very personal level, the worry that delay brings because of a non-accident related experience I had that I'll now share with you to illustrate the point. Six months after my son was born, I noticed that I had a stiff neck that wouldn't get better. For two weeks, I sought out massage and chiropractic treatment, but nothing seemed to help. Then, while on a trip with my family to Portland, I got a fever and had a terrible headache with sharp pain in my ear. We made it home (my wife drove), but I was still very sick. I stayed home from work to recuperate, and after a few days, I seemed to be doing better. The next morning, I was thinking I was nearly ready to return to work when my wife asked me in an alarmed voice, "What happened to your face?" She told me I looked like I'd had a stroke. I checked the mirror, and sure enough, the entire right side of my face was paralyzed.

Can you imagine the terror I felt? Was I having a stroke? Was there something wrong with my brain? Would my face ever return to normal? I am a trial lawyer. I make a living telling other peoples' stories and being their advocate. How could I do that with a face that was so deformed? My wife rushed me to the emergency room, and after several hours, I was diagnosed with shingles in my ear, which had caused inflammation, resulting in damage to the nerve that controls the right side of my face. The first doctor I saw wanted to do brain surgery to relieve the pressure on the nerve, but I sought a second opinion from a top neurologist who prescribed a more conservative course of action.

As I began my treatment, I could not close my right eye, pucker my lips, or even smile. I had to be careful when eating and drinking because I couldn't keep anything in my mouth. I was determined to make a full recovery and to do so as fast as I could. I launched myself into steroids and anti-virals for the shingles, and every kind of therapy I could think of to restore function to my face. I tried physical therapy, acupuncture, chiropractic, and cold lasers. I even tried hypnotherapy and practiced visualizing my face fully healed.

For the first several weeks, I could not see any change. I started making a weekly video of my face to track the progress, and slowly but surely, the function began to return to my face. Within months, the injury was hardly noticeable, and over time, I made an almost complete recovery, but while I was waiting for it to get better, it seemed like forever, and it magnified all of the doubts and worries I was experiencing. The same feelings can arise while you're awaiting your trial to begin. Just know that someday, it will all be over with and you'll be looking back upon it.

SORTING THINGS OUT

Sometimes, the delay results not from the system, but from the particular facts of the case. For example, in 2010, Edward Black stepped off of a King County METRO bus into a hole in the parking strip adjacent to the sidewalk. He fell and ruptured his patellar tendon, requiring reconstructive surgery and months of rehab. Edward came to me for assistance. When I explored the possibility of settling Edward's claim, it became clear that nobody was willing to accept responsibility for his injury. The adjacent property owner (a corporation) denied it was its responsibility and pointed the finger at the City of Seattle. The City claimed it had no notice of the dangerous condition (the hole in the ground) and blamed the landowner. Both the City and the landowner blamed King County for dropping off a passenger at a dangerous location, and King County blamed the City and the landowner. In this situation, a negotiated settlement was all but impossible, so we filed a lawsuit and named the City of Seattle, the adjacent landowner and its tenant, and King County as the defendants.

Of course, once a lawsuit is filed, every party gets to conduct discovery on every other party, which means interrogatories (written questions), depositions (in-person questions), and production of documents, photos, and other evidence. Eventually, after several months, each of the defendants filed motions for Summary Judgment, asking the judge to rule as a matter of law that it had no responsibility for the injury. Our response was that we didn't care *which* entity was ultimately responsible, only that *some* entity be held responsible for this incident, which was clearly not our client's fault. The judge dismissed the claims against the City and the landowner, leaving only the claims against King County.

Once King County was the only defendant left, I was able to negotiate a fair settlement of Edward's claims pretty quickly, but as long as there were multiple defendants, each pointing the finger at the other, settlement was impossible. The process of eliminating defendants and determining the party with ultimate responsibility took more than a year. During that time, Edward continued to suffer from pain and disability in his knee, and he continued to have money problems as a result of his medical bills and inability to work.

The pace of our civil justice system can be slow—sometimes excruciatingly slow—but it is still the best system I know of to hold people or entities responsible when their carelessness results in injuries to others.

CONCLUSION

There's just no getting around it. The litigation process is slow. In my office, we are committed to regular communication with our clients, even if just to inform them that nothing has changed. We understand that waiting months or even years to get your day in court is unfair, and it can be extremely frustrating. We try to antici-pate the delays and to explain to our clients, with as much certainty as we can, what will happen and how long it will take. We find that this communication can lessen the anxiety and frustration that ac-companies the necessary delays in the process. But delay isn't the worst part of the process. In the next chapter, we will discuss how the insurance company lawyers get to investigate your personal and medical history as they look for ways to defeat your claims against them.

CHAPTER 18
EXPOSING YOUR LIFE

Once you expose your private life, if you give one little bit,
the floodgates are open and everyone's got a free range for you.

— Jason Statham

In the last chapter, I discussed the slow pace of the civil justice system and how that pace can result from the nature of the system itself or the specific facts of your case. The delays inherent in litigation can be frustrating and even painful, but they give you and your lawyer time to prepare your case for trial. Perhaps even more difficult is the intrusive nature of the litigation process. We have previously discussed the discovery process, but you may not be prepared for just how deep the other side can dig in search of a defense to your claims. When you make a claim for a bodily injury, you are placing your physical condition at issue. That makes your entire health history fair game. The insurance company can ask you questions about prior injuries and illnesses, and it can pore over your medical records, looking for something—anything—it can use against you. It can ask you questions about your work history, marital history, mental state, prior claims or lawsuits, and much more. A good lawyer can protect you from the worst of this, but discovery in a civil suit is inevitable, and for many people, it can be extremely unpleasant. In some cases, it can even lead to the destruction of your claim.

THE PROTECTIVE ORDER

One of my clients, Andy Smythe, suffered a major injury when another driver fell asleep at the wheel, crossed the center line, and hit Andy's car head-on. Andy's body was thrown forward and his hands flexed on the steering wheel, causing damage to his right wrist that compressed the nerves going into his hand. After months of physical therapy without any improvement, Andy had surgery to decompress the nerves in his wrist. Even after the surgery, he continued to have problems.

After the insurance company refused to make a fair offer on Andy's claim, we filed a lawsuit and began to prepare for trial. Among the discovery requests we received from the defense were requests to obtain all of Andy's medical records for the five years before the accident. In general, this request was fair. Since we were claiming the defendant had caused injuries not just to Andy's wrist, but also to his neck and back, the defense had a right to see for itself whether similar issues existed in the recent past that may not have been the result of this accident.

The problem was that Andy was in the middle of a nasty custody battle, so there were records he did not want his ex-wife to see or be able to access. His concern was that the defense might obtain sensitive records and file them as exhibits or evidence in the auto case, making them part of the public record. He even considered abandoning his claim just to prevent his medical records from becoming public. People may have other reasons for wanting to keep their medical records confidential, especially if they aren't directly relevant to the injuries being claimed.

In this case, because the concern was not about the defense attorney seeing the records, but rather that they might become public, I approached the defense attorney and asked him to agree to a protective order. A protective order is a ruling by the court that certain discovery does not need to take place or that certain records will remain confidential. In this case, we agreed that the defense attorney's office would keep the requested records private, and that if it intended to offer them as exhibits or evidence, it would advise us first and give us an opportunity to have the judge determine whether the records were relevant and necessary. Finally, we agreed that if the judge did allow the records into evidence, they could be entered as sealed documents, which are not accessible by the general public. This agreement addressed my client's concerns while allowing the defense to conduct the discovery it needed.

SKELETONS IN THE CLOSET

Andy had reasons to protect the confidentiality of his medical records that had nothing to do with his claim. Other clients sometimes want to keep their medical history a secret (even from their own lawyers) for other reasons. Usually they fail, and by keeping secrets from their lawyers, they increase the risk that their cases will self-destruct in a moment of discovery or inadvertent revelation.

I always tell my clients to discuss anything with me that might be relevant to their claims. I want to know anything they might be embarrassed about and anything they fear might hurt their claims. I ask for this information not to make my clients uncomfortable, but so I can prepare an effective strategy to deal with facts that might be less than ideal. If the first time I hear about a potentially-damaging fact is during my client's deposition, or worse yet, at an arbitration hearing or trial, it's usually too late to do anything about it. I've seen that happen several times.

Once I had a client hire me for an uninsured motorist claim involving severe back injuries that required disc surgery. It looked like a solid claim until his insurance carrier provided me with his prior medical records, which documented that a physician had recommended spinal surgery two weeks *before* the accident. As a result, I was forced to drop the claim. Had the client explained the situation earlier, I might have been able to salvage some portion of the claim for the worsening of a pre-existing condition, but by the time I discovered the information, it was too late to do anything about it.

I have had clients hide prior drug and alcohol addictions, severe injuries, health conditions, involuntary commitments for mental health issues, criminal convictions, multiple prior lawsuits, and more. None of these things, by itself, is necessarily fatal to an injury claim. If somebody was negligent and caused you harm, you are entitled to compensation. But if you try to misrepresent your physical or mental condition prior to the accident, or if you get caught in a lie, even a valid claim can disintegrate very quickly.

IRRELEVANT PRIOR RECORDS

Sometimes, prior medical records that have nothing to do with the case get into evidence and muck things up for your claim. As discussed in previous chapters, claims adjusters and defense attorneys will latch onto anything that can create doubt or confusion regarding your claim. Sometimes, all they have to do is get an unrelated page of your medical records into evidence and let the jury's imagination take over.

In Chapter 16, I discussed a medical malpractice trial I assisted in. This case involved a doctor's negligent failure to diagnose and treat a potentially fatal condition in an expecting mother. The condition, called twin-twin transfusion syndrome, causes unborn twins to get an uneven blood supply. One twin gets too much, and the other literally starves to death. If caught early, this condition can be treated and reversed, but in this case, the doctors failed to see the signs, so treatment was delayed. Ultimately, one twin died and the other was born with profound brain damage.

Among the hundreds of pages of medical records that became part of the evidence in that case was a reference to an episode of chlamydia, a sexually transmitted disease that the mom had contracted and for which she had received treatment as a teenager. Now, I don't know how this record ended up being left in evidence. I was a very young attorney and my boss was handling all of the arguments on evidence. I don't recall any pre-trial argument about it. In any case, it was one of the medical records the jury was allowed to consider in its deliberations.

It is important to note that no doctor from either side ever suggested that an STD could cause twin-twin transfusion syndrome or was in any way responsible for the harm suffered by the twins and their mother. However, the jury members, on their own, found this one mention of an unrelated medical condition and ran with it. A few of them suggested that this disease may have caused the condition. Ultimately, the jury ruled for the defense, so our client got nothing.

This outcome was heartbreaking for our client, but it was a valuable learning experience for me. I learned that juries can be unpredictable and they don't always limit their deliberations to the evidence and testimony presented. I learned that every word of the medical records is important, even if it seems completely unrelated to the injury being claimed, and I learned that prior medical history can have a profound impact on a case's outcome.

CONCLUSION

The litigation process is not for the faint hearted. It is time consuming and emotionally grueling. As a plaintiff, you can expect the defense attorney to probe your past—not just your medical history, but your work history, family history, criminal history, and anything else it can use to cause confusion and doubt among the jury members. It may be that something in your history will prevent you from making a full recovery in your case—or it may not have any impact at all. The best way to know is to be painfully honest and thorough with your attorney. If there is something— anything—that would embarrass you if people found out, or something you worry might affect your claim, you must tell your lawyer. Having this information early in the process is crucial to preparing a proper claim and anticipating the arguments that might be made by the insurance company. You might think you can keep your secret through the litigation process, and you might be right, but you're probably wrong, and the attempt to conceal the truth could destroy your case.

Take a moment now and use the lines below to write down any issues or concerns you have that you think could affect your case. Make sure you share them with your attorney. Include anything you'd be embarrassed or concerned to have the jury discover. Make sure you share all of these concerns with your attorney. They'll probably be no big deal, but trying to keep them a secret could result in a disaster.

_____

_____

_____

_____

_____

_____

_____

_____

_____

_____

CHAPTER 19

EXPLORING ALTERNATIVES TO TRIAL

As a peace-maker the lawyer has a superior opportunity of being a good man. There will still be business enough.

— Abraham Lincoln

In the previous chapter, I discussed the impact that your past can have on your legal claim and the dangers that skeletons in your closet could pose to your lawsuit, but even if you have nothing in your past that could harm your case, there are many good reasons to avoid trial. Trials are risky and unpredictable. No matter how much of a lock your case seems, there is always a possibility that you will lose and get significantly less than what you want, or even nothing at all. Trials are time-consuming. In King County, Washington, it commonly takes more than eighteen months from the filing of a lawsuit to get your day in court. During that time, you and your lawyers have to plan and prepare, and submit to written questions, depositions, and medical examinations. Trials are expensive. The insurance companies have unlimited resources, but you do not. A simple trial can easily cost over $10,000, and a more complex case could cost $100,000 or more. In addition to filing fees, legal messengers, and court reporter fees, there is the cost of expert witnesses, report preparation, travel, preparation of exhibits, and more. If you lose at trial, your contingent fee lawyer doesn't get paid, but you are still on the hook for the expenses. Sometimes, going to trial is absolutely worth the risk, and sometimes, the insurance company leaves you no choice but to fight to the bitter end, but there are tools available that can increase your chances of reaching a satisfactory conclusion to your case before trial. These tools are generally referred to as alternative dispute resolution (ADR). The three primary forms of ADR are negotiation, mediation, and arbitration.

DO AS WE SAY—WE'RE ECUADOR

Before I transferred to Yale, I obtained my Associates degree at Rockland Community College in Suffern, New York. While at Rockland, I was Student Senate Treasurer and Chair of the Political Activities Club, but the position I enjoyed most was President of the Model United Nations Club. We would meet regularly to learn how a deliberative body operates. We drafted resolutions, practiced parliamentary procedure, and engaged in sometimes heated debates.

Every year, a National Intercollegiate Model United Nations is held. The year I attended, my school was assigned Ecuador. We were tasked with learning all there is to know about this small South American country, from its economy to its geography. Mostly, we were advised to find out what issues were important to Ecuador in the field of international relations. In preparing, we learned an interesting fact. Ecuador was one of the few countries in the world that claimed territorial rights to the geosynchronous orbit above its national boundaries. That means it asserted the right to stop you from placing a satellite in orbit over it.

When our club arrived at the Grand Hyatt Hotel in Manhattan, the whole scene was overwhelming. There were thousands of kids from hundreds of schools—each representing a country. George-town University represented the United States. Harvard was the Soviet Union (it was 1988 and the Cold War was still on). Rockland Community College was Ecuador. Nobody cared about Ecuador, and nobody had any reason to listen to our concerns, so how could we possibly hope to accomplish any of our goals?

We decided as a team to focus all of our attention on the geosynchronous orbit issue. We developed a strategy that involved ceaselessly learning what other delegations wanted and offering our support in exchange for their support in protecting Ecuador's rights to the space above its borders. There were hundreds of proposed resolutions. Most died in committee, but many passed through to the General Assembly. There were resolutions on trade, human rights, the environment, and just about every other issue you could imagine. One of the resolutions that made it through committee was an unlikely proposal made by a small South American nation to protect its sovereignty over its orbital space.

None of the other schools really had a position on our issue. They probably hadn't considered the issue at all before we brought it up. We used that to our advantage by finding out what was important to them and trading our support for theirs. After all, we were Ecuador. We really didn't care about global CO_2 emissions or trade embargoes. Ultimately, I was able to make a rousing speech to the Assembly on the rights of all people, and the justice of our position, but it wasn't my speech that won the day. It was the tireless work of listening to the other participants, finding out what they wanted, and giving them a reason to support our cause. In the end, our resolution passed and we won an award as one of the best delegations at the event.

When it comes to your personal injury claim, you are Ecuador. The big insurance companies are the superpowers, so they don't care about you. So how do you get what you want—a fair recovery for your injuries? You have to listen to them and find out what they want; then you need to make a compelling case that it is in their own best interest to offer you a fair settlement. That's what negotiation is. I prepare your case for trial so the insurance company can see the risk it faces from a jury. It is only after I persuade the insurance company of its risk that it will make you a reasonable offer. Sometimes, all it takes is a well-prepared demand. Sometimes, the insurance company needs to hear from the experts hired on your behalf. Sometimes, nothing we say ourselves is enough to persuade the insurance company, but hearing it from an impartial outsider (a mediator) will get it to change its tune. Finally, sometimes we can have a neutral decision maker (an arbitrator) decide for us what your claim is worth without the need to go to trial. Throughout this process, it is our single-minded focus to get the best possible recovery for your claim, just like it was my club's single-minded focus to get support for our orbit issue when we were Ecuador at the Model United Nations.

NEGOTIATION

Much of what I've already shared in this book is about the negotiation process. From the day you hire me, I am thinking ahead to trial. What are the strengths of your claim? What are the weaknesses? What will the insurance company try to use to reduce your recovery? By anticipating these issues, I can address them early so they don't prevent you from getting a fair recovery.

In almost every case, once you have completed your treatment, we prepare a comprehensive demand package. The purpose of the demand package is threefold. First, we want to show the insurance company that your claim is serious. Even if you did not suffer a catastrophic injury, every injury is serious. Every injury disrupts your life, and every injury deserves to be compensated. Second, we want to show the insurance company that *we* are serious. A professional and complete presentation shows the insurance company that we understand the issues in your claim and we know how to make the most of your case. This is important because if the insurance company doesn't perceive the risk to it, it will never make you a fair offer. And that is why the third objective of the demand is to show that we are willing to go all the way if necessary to get what you deserve.

In the demand package, we typically give the insurance company thirty days to review your case and make an offer. If it refuses to make an offer, usually our only option is to file a lawsuit, but it almost always responds within the thirty days. Sadly, most of the time, its opening offer is insultingly low. It's not that it thinks your claim has no value. It's just playing the insurance company game, trying to scare you into settling your claim for less than it is worth. I advise my clients never, never, ever to accept the insurance company's opening offer. Instead, we discuss the strengths and weaknesses of your claim and the risks to each side in an effort to find an acceptable middle ground. Because the insurance company knows that if we don't settle your claim, it will go to trial, we are usually able to reach a fair outcome.

MEDIATION

Sometimes, mostly due to lack of trust, neither side is willing to make its best offer to get the case resolved. In such a case, a good mediator can make all the difference in the world. Although there are different types of mediation, the kind I find most useful and prefer to use is a form of "shuttle diplomacy." In this arrangement, we sit in one conference room while the insurance company, its lawyers, and its adjusters sit in another room. The mediator, often a retired judge or a very experienced attorney, reviews the facts of the case in advance and then listens to each side. A good mediator makes sure that both sides feel heard and respected.

After listening to both sides and understanding what each side hopes to accomplish, the mediator explains his own evaluation of the claim, including its strengths, weaknesses, and anticipated value. Often, the mediator has to go back and forth between the parties for hours or even days, and sometimes, even with a mediator's help, the case can't be settled. But even if the case is not resolved, a mediation can help us understand the arguments being made by the insurance company, and it can narrow the gap between our position and theirs. Often, a case settles within days or weeks of a "failed" mediation.

ARBITRATION

As with mediation, different kinds of arbitration exist. For our purposes, the most important distinction is between binding and non-binding arbitration. Just as it sounds, in binding arbitration, the arbitrator's decision is final. There is no appeal, no escape. The parties are bound by the decision. Equally obvious, in non-binding arbitration, an unhappy party can appeal the arbitrator's decision to a higher authority—usually a court.

In the State of Washington, we have a mandatory arbitration program that allows any injured person who is willing to limit his recovery to $50,000 to demand arbitration. As I write this, the State Legislature is considering a bill that would raise the limit to $100,000. There are many benefits to this program. Arbitration is faster, cheaper, and less emotionally taxing than trial. The arbitrators are attorneys who generally understand the issues involved in your claim and are mostly committed to giving you a fair hearing. When you place your case into arbitration in King County, you can expect a decision within four to six months versus the eighteen months it can take to get to a jury trial. However, this arbitration is not binding, and either side can appeal the decision and demand a jury trial.

The other kind of arbitration has to be agreed to by the parties.

They can agree to any terms they want, such as a minimum and maximum award (generally referred to as a high-low arbitration) and limitations on discovery, such as depositions and interrogatories. These are almost always binding on the parties, although they could agree in advance on a method of appeal if they want.

Even the most complex arbitration can be preferable to a jury trial because it can help you avoid some of the delay, expense, and procedural difficulty of trying your case before a jury. But sometimes, your case is too big, the insurance company is too unreasonable, and alternative dispute resolution fails, leaving you no option but to go to trial.

CONCLUSION

Many alternatives exist to trial, and most of them can result in a faster, less expensive, and more certain outcome than submitting your claims to a jury. A good personal injury lawyer will explain all of these options to you and discuss which ones are right for you and your claim. In the end, your claim may or may not settle, but knowing you've tried everything before going to trial can make the decision to try the case feel better. In the next chapter, we will discuss the final steps you and your lawyer will have to take leading up to trial.

CHAPTER 20

GEARING UP FOR TRIAL

You don't climb mountains without a team, you don't climb mountains without being fit, you don't climb mountains without being prepared and you don't climb mountains without balancing the risks and rewards. And you never climb a mountain on accident— it has to be intentional.

— Mark Udall

We've talked about what to do before you ever get hurt in an accident. We've talked about what to do at the scene and immediately following the accident. We've talked about injuries, doctor visits, insurance companies, recorded statements, demand packages, and mediation. But after all of that, if your claim still hasn't been resolved, you and your lawyer had better be prepared for trial. Trying a case is like climbing a mountain—you can't just find yourself there and expect to win. It takes months, and sometimes years, of preparation. It takes a team of attorneys, support staff, doctors, expert witnesses, and family members. A good lawyer begins preparing for your trial the day you hire her. That way, every step—

whether discussing your injuries with your doctor, speaking to the claims adjuster, or taking the defendant's deposition—is always taken with an eye toward trial. This approach not only gives you the best chance to win at trial, but it also makes it less likely that you will have to go to trial. A well-prepared and worked-up claim is much more likely to generate meaningful offers of settlement. But at this point, we're done talking about settlement. Your case has not settled, so now we're headed to trial.

FINDING THE RIGHT EXPERT

Earlier, I mentioned my client who fractured her heel on the brake pedal of her car when she was T-boned at an intersection. Although the fracture was very serious, she was diabetic and had significant loss of sensation in her feet. The foot would not support her weight, but she still waited three full days before going to the doctor. When she finally went to her primary care physician, the doctor misdiagnosed the problem as a complication of diabetes rather than an acute injury from the accident. Because of the improper diagnosis, she did not get the appropriate treatment, and she spent more than a year completely unable to walk. Can you imagine?

When we filed the claim, the insurance company insisted that the first doctor was right—it was simply a complication of her diabetes. It claimed that if she had really broken her foot in the accident, she would have been unable to deal with the pain and would have sought immediate help. The insurance company even hired an orthopedic surgeon (one of the usual suspects who regularly testifies for insurance companies) who said there was *no way* the injury happened in the accident. I knew we needed to be prepared for this argument, so I spent hours speaking to the surgeon who ultimately repaired the damaged foot. I asked him every question I could think of about the injury and its cause, the course of treatment, and the ultimate surgical fix. I reviewed x-rays and read textbooks. I learned everything I could about this kind of injury and the injury the insurance company claimed she had.

Ultimately, the doctor testified brilliantly that the injury could *only* have been caused by the accident. He explained clearly and confidently using simple visual aids and x-rays. It was because of the months of preparation put into this case that I was able to recover almost $400,000 for this client in a case where the insurance company initially refused to make an offer at all.

LINING UP THE WITNESSES

Medical testimony is important in trial, but it is not enough to win a full recovery. As I tell my clients, the true value of your case lies not in your medical bills, but in how your injuries affected your life. No matter how experienced or well-educated your doctor may be, he can never adequately explain how you experienced your injuries and how they affected your life and your family. The people who need to do that are you and your friends and family members—the people closest to you. These are the people who knew you before you were hurt and who know how your injuries affected your life.

I won't be able to parade fifty witnesses to talk about what a great person you are and how devastating your injuries were, so I will need to identify which witnesses to call. I need to interview them and find out exactly what they know and what they will say. Finally, I need to decide which questions should be addressed by each witness to communicate your unique story most effectively to the jury.

Sometimes, the person who knows the most about you isn't the best witness. Some people are shy and get nervous when speaking in front of strangers. Others can be scattered or disorganized in their thoughts. I help the witnesses understand why they are testifying, prepare them to help tell your story, and prepare them to deal with cross-examination by the insurance company lawyers, but once they take the stand, they are more or less on their own. It's the lawyer's job to call the right witnesses in the right order and ask them the right questions to help the jury really understand what you've been through.

Of course, the most important witness in a personal injury claim is the plaintiff. Nobody, and I mean nobody, knows exactly what you've been through except you. I've been injured in an accident, so I know what it's like to be hurt, but I can't get into your skin, and neither can your husband or wife, your parents or children, or your friends. Ultimately, to get a good result, you are going to have to be prepared to bare your soul to a jury of strangers. It's not enough to tell them how you felt physically. You need to talk about how it made you feel emotionally. You need to talk about your fear that you will never be the same person, your feelings of inadequacy stemming from not being able to take care of your family, your depression about gaining weight, your frustration with all the appointments, or your inability to do the most basic things like make your bed or do the laundry. You will need to tell the jury about how your injuries affected your personal life, your home life, your work life, and your social life. And you will need to be prepared for the insurance company's lawyer to dismiss everything you say and try to paint you as a complainer, a malingerer, an exaggerator, and even a liar.

With the right expert and lay witnesses lined up, we're almost ready for trial, but we need to give the jury members something to hold in their hands and look at. We need to prepare and organize the exhibits.

PREPARING THE EXHIBITS

If you have a good lawyer, the trial exhibits are ready long before trial. The exhibits are physical items such as documents, bills, charts, photographs, or other items that will be entered into evidence at your trial. Along with the testimony of the witnesses, the exhibits are the only things the jury is supposed to consider when deciding your case, so it's important to get them right.

In a case of disputed liability, exhibits will likely include photos of the accident scene. They could also include documents showing the patterns of traffic lights, weather reports, and more. Reports of accident reconstructionists or other investigators are usually not entered into evidence. Rather, these experts testify in person and explain their opinions. Often, we will use exhibits to illustrate the testimony of an expert, especially if it is complex.

Exhibits can also be used to help the jury understand your injuries and medical treatment. We can use some or all of your medical records and bills. We can use illustrations of body parts and medical procedures. Often, we will use models or illustrations to help explain the testimony of your doctor or the medical experts.

Finally, exhibits can be used to document other damages such as lost wages, cancelled trips, purchases of special equipment, and more.

Sometimes, it is better to enter all of the documents into evidence, but sometimes, it can be to your advantage to use the witness testimony to establish the case and to have only selected documents entered into evidence. It is your lawyer's job to determine which exhibits are necessary to prove your case, which witness can provide testimony about that exhibit, and how the exhibits can be presented along with the witness testimony in a way that maximizes the effectiveness of telling your story, and, ultimately, maximizes your chances of getting a fair recovery at trial.

The exhibits are generally identified and numbered before the trial even begins, so your lawyer had better know well in advance how she's going to tell your story and what exhibits she'll need to do so.

OTHER PRETRIAL MATTERS

All kinds of other procedural requirements and arguments happen before trial. The lawyers argue motions about what evidence the jury can see and what should be withheld. They argue about how the judge should instruct the jury both before the trial begins and at the conclusion of the evidence. They may ask the judge to rule on some or all of the issues in the case before the trial begins.

All of these arguments are made in writing and then argued in front of the trial judge, who makes the final decision.

CONCLUSION

The discovery period is drawn out and passes slowly. Hopefully, your lawyer is using this time to develop a strategy for trying your case and is mapping out the witnesses and exhibits he will need to present to the jury. Once discovery ends, the process speeds up. This pretrial phase is filled with intense preparation and goes by much faster.

Up to this point, we've discussed every aspect of your personal injury claim except for the trial. As I've said before, most claims settle because most lawyers only take strong claims. But regardless of the strength of your case, sometimes the insurance companies give us no choice but to go to trial. When that happens, you'd better be ready to go. In this chapter, I discussed the final steps you and your lawyer will take before you enter the courtroom for your trial. In the next chapter, we will talk about the trial itself—what it looks and feels like, and what will happen within those courtroom walls.

CHAPTER 21

HAVING YOUR DAY IN COURT

There is no such thing as an impartial jury because there are no impartial people. There are people that argue on the web for hours about who their favorite character on Friends *is.*

— Jon Stewart

You were hurt in an accident maybe years ago. You've been through months or years of pain, disability, and doctor visits. You've missed work or maybe lost your job. Your family life has been strained, and you still might not be back to 100 percent. You tried to deal with the insurance company yourself, but you realized you were in over your head, so you made the wise choice to hire an experienced personal injury lawyer. You've been through negotiations and the insurance company refused to take your claim seriously. You agreed with your lawyer to file a lawsuit (which seems like years ago), but you never really thought you'd have to go to trial. Your life has been an open book, with strangers poring through your medical records and your whole life while they looked for arguments to use against you at trial. You've been to mediation, where the insurance company may have increased its offer, but still not to anywhere near what your claim is worth. You've waited and waited for months while it seemed like nothing was happening (even though your lawyer was likely hard at work the whole time). You've helped your lawyer identify which witnesses to call, and you've prepared yourself to give your own testimony.

Finally, it's time for your day in court.

THE BROAD OVERVIEW

First, let me say this: I could write a whole book on trials. I could go into the nuances of trial strategy, the opening statement, witness examinations, objections, summation, and issues that arise during a trial. I could tell story after story of surprise testimony, unreasonable judges, unusual jurors, and outrageous outcomes. Maybe that will be my next book, but it's not this book. If you've done everything right in your injury claim, there's a very good chance you'll never get to this point. If you do end up in trial, this chapter will give you a very broad idea of what to expect.

As I see it, the trial is divided into five phases: preliminary matters, opening statements, case in chief, defense, and summation. Each phase is important enough to make or break your case, so your attorney must understand and be an effective advocate in all five phases. I will give a brief summary of each:

1. **Preliminary matters.**

In the previous chapter, I discussed arguments over jury instructions and what evidence the jury gets to see (motions in limine). While these are pre-trial matters, they are generally argued and decided by the judge on the morning of trial. That means, before we even get started, you are sitting around while the lawyers argue about technicalities. These technicalities are immensely important.

A subtle change in the language of the jury instructions could easily change the outcome of a case. Just imagine the difference between these two instructions: "You shall consider all of the evidence presented at trial" or "You may consider all of the evidence presented at trial." Your lawyer has already proposed a set of instructions to the judge, as has the opposing lawyer. After brief argument, the judge will make the final decision and the instructions will be prepared. It is essential that your lawyer know what the instructions will be before he starts presenting evidence. The instructions establish what needs to be proven and by what standard. Without knowing and fully understanding the instructions, no lawyer can effectively present your case.

The issue of what evidence the jury gets to hear is equally important. People often develop opinions about major trials based on what they see on television, but it's very likely that those jurors didn't see the same information you did. Many rules of evidence limit or prevent the presentation of information to the jury. For instance, if you slipped on defective stairs and the property owner subsequently fixed the stairs, you cannot use that information to show that the stairs were defective in the first place. The policy behind this rule is to avoid discouraging property owners from fixing dangerous situations, but it sure can make your case more difficult. One very important rule is that the jury doesn't get to hear anything about the fact that the defendant has insurance to cover your loss. Even though your whole claim has been against the insurance company—the insurance company hired the lawyer, and when you win, it is the insurance company that will pay you—when you go to trial, it is you against the other driver. Any mention of the insurance company is strictly forbidden. You can imagine that a jury would be more sympathetic to the poor defendant, who had a moment of inattention and wrecked your life, than it would to the big bad insurance company.

Motions in limine can work to your advantage as well. The insurance company is not allowed to present evidence of your prior, unrelated medical history. It cannot offer information about your criminal history, except in very narrow circumstances. I have been able to prevent it from showing photos of minor property damage, successfully arguing that no reliable scientific correlation exists between property damage and bodily injury.

All of these matters usually take the first morning of trial, and then it's on to voir dire, or jury selection. Here, the lawyers narrow a pool of fifty or sixty potential jurors to the final twelve-person jury. First, the judge asks everyone some general questions, and then the lawyers get to ask questions. Each lawyer gets to excuse jurors for cause if their answers indicate that they have a prejudice or are unable to be impartial, and each lawyer gets a few strikes without needing to give a reason. Once the jury is selected, we're finally ready to go.

2. Opening Statements

The opening statements are where the lawyers get to tell the jurors what the case is about and what evidence they will hear. Your lawyer's opening statement sets the tone for the whole trial. One item I start preparing the day a client hires me is the story of the case and how it can be explained in a clear and compelling way.

Compare the following statements:

"On November 15, 2012, at 8:34 a.m., Jane MacDonald was crossing 45th Street NE at the intersection of NE Meridian Avenue when she was struck by the defendant's black 2013 Cadillac CTS after he ran a red light. She suffered a broken hip and torn ligaments in her shoulder. She required surgery on her hip and spent six days at Harborview Medical Center. After six months of rehabilitation, her doctors concluded that she had a 6 percent permanent disability. Jane's medical bills were $65,000, and we are seeking an additional $200,000 for her pain and suffering."

Or

"November 15, 2012 started out just like any other day for Jane MacDonald. She got her kids onto the school bus, kissed her husband goodbye, and began the twenty-minute walk to her church, where she volunteered every Wednesday at a local food bank. Jane walked the same route every week, and she knew that crossing 45th Street could be dangerous, so she made sure she had a walk signal, she looked both ways, and she carefully began to cross in the crosswalk. Little did she know that her life was about to change in ways she couldn't even imagine. In a moment of carelessness, the defendant made a right on red without making sure the crosswalk was clear. The front bumper of his Cadillac hit Jane just above her right knee and threw her to the pavement, causing serious and permanent injuries. In the next few days, you will hear from Jane's doctors about the catastrophic nature of her injuries. You will hear from Jane's husband and her pastor about how these injuries turned her life upside down. Finally, you will hear from Jane herself, who will tell you in her own words how she coped with this unexpected catastrophe. At the conclusion of the trial, I will ask you to make a monetary award to Jane. It's impossible to place a dollar value on what Jane went through, but that is exactly what you are being asked to do."

Do you see the difference? It is the lawyer's job to use the evidence and the witnesses to tell the story of what happened and to explain why the plaintiff is entitled to money. While the insurance company views the case as medical bills and diagnosis codes, in order to prevail at trial, we must get the jury to identify with you as a human being with a real life and a real story to tell. Of course, once a lawyer makes a statement in opening, he'd better be able to back it up with evidence. If I were to tell the jury that the Cadillac struck

Jane above the knee, but it actually struck her below the knee, that could damage my credibility with the jury, and it could hurt her chances to make a good recovery.

Once your lawyer completes his opening statement, the insurance company lawyer gets a turn. The job of the defense at trial is not to prove anything. It is instead to create confusion and doubt. I often describe the plaintiff's burden of proof as blowing up a balloon. Each fact and each piece of evidence is another puff of air. When you fully inflate the balloon, you win. But while you're blowing up the balloon, the insurance company lawyer is throwing darts. If one of those darts hits and the balloon bursts, you lose.

If the defense can get the jury to start thinking about irrelevant issues or start questioning the injured person's character rather than keeping the focus on what happened to her, it wins. It may blame the doctor for over-treating. It may blame the injuries on some other incident. It may deny that the injury even took place. Just like the plaintiff, it will have to back up these statements with expert or other witness testimony, but there's always a doctor willing to say what the insurance companies want. Some doctors make millions of dollars each year doing exactly that.

Once the opening statements have been made, it's time to begin presenting the evidence. It's time to move to the next phase, the case in chief.

3. The Case in Chief

In any civil trial, the burden of proof is on the plaintiff. That means the injured person must prove the elements of the claim by a preponderance of the evidence. In all negligence cases, the elements of the case are duty, breach, causation, and damages. It's not enough to show that you were hurt. You have to show that the defendant had a duty to avoid hurting you and that he failed to meet that duty. We prove these elements through the evidence. That is the case in chief.

Before the trial, your lawyer already decided which exhibits he needs the jury to see and which witness he will use to authenticate and explain each exhibit. Unless pre-admitted, every exhibit needs to be demonstrated as authentic and relevant by a competent witness before the judge will allow it to be admitted into evidence.

At this point in the trial, you'll probably hear the expected words: "Your Honor, the Plaintiff calls her first witness."

One by one, your lawyer will ask questions designed to elicit the witness's knowledge—his piece of the story—in his own words, and to introduce the exhibits that support and reinforce that testimony. For example, an eyewitness might be used to introduce photos of the accident scene. A doctor could be used to introduce medical records, and a family member could be used to introduce photos showing Jane's impairment.

After your lawyer questions each witness, the insurance company's lawyer gets to cross-examine her. Unlike the direct examination, in cross-examination, the lawyer is allowed to ask leading questions such as: "You weren't even looking at the intersection when the accident took place, were you?" or "You've complained of knee problems for years prior to this incident, haven't you?" Your lawyer should make sure the witnesses know to expect these questions and to answer them honestly and without excuse, explanation, or argument. If additional information is necessary to give the jury a true understanding of what happened, your lawyer gets another chance to let the witness clarify his testimony on redirect. Arguing or explaining, and especially lying under oath, are some of the worst things a witness can do.

After your lawyer has called the last witness and has entered all of the evidence that he needs to prove your case, he will rest. He will literally say: "Your Honor, the Plaintiff rests." At this point, you can expect a motion from the insurance company lawyer to dismiss all of your claims based on the lawyer's failure to prove one or more of the elements in the case in chief. The judge will always consider such a motion, but if you have a good case and a halfway decent lawyer, the motion should be denied.

After the plaintiff has rested and the motion to dismiss is denied, the roles are reversed and the insurance company lawyer gets to call witnesses. That is the fourth phase, the defense.

4. The Defense

Just like in the case in chief, in the defense, the insurance company lawyer calls witnesses and offers exhibits into evidence, and your attorney gets to cross-examine the witnesses.

Typical witnesses the insurance company might call are: 1) an accident reconstructionist to deny that the accident happened or to dispute some aspect of your story; 2) a doctor to question the seriousness of your injuries or the judgment of your health care providers; 3) the defendant to deny liability, or if admitting liability, then denying that it was anywhere near as serious as you make it out to be. Of course, your lawyer should have taken depositions of all of these witnesses months earlier and should be prepared for whatever it is they're going to say.

Remember, the defense doesn't need to prove anything. It is its job to create confusion and doubt. If the jury is confused, then it is less likely to find that you proved your case. It is your lawyer's job to avoid getting distracted by collateral issues and to keep the jury focused on what is important in the case.

Once the insurance company lawyer has called her last witness, she will rest, and then your lawyer gets to call rebuttal witnesses or recall a previous witness to rebut something that was said by one of the insurance company's witnesses. Finally, all of the exhibits have been admitted, all of the witnesses have testified, and each side has rested. Now it's time for summation, or closing argument.

5. Summation

A summation is exactly what it sounds like. It is a summary of the evidence that the jury has seen and heard, and it is an explanation (if necessary) of why that evidence supports a verdict in your favor. Remember those jury instructions we discussed earlier? Typically, the judge will read those instructions to the jury before summation. That way the jury will know what to listen for in the lawyers' arguments. Then, as with the opening statements, your lawyer goes first and the insurance company lawyer goes second.

Unlike the opening statement, the summation is an argument; that's why it's called a closing argument. It reminds the jury members what they have heard from the witnesses and how that evidence supports a particular element of the claim, such as damages. Different lawyers have different styles of closing argument, and the presentation changes from case to case. The gist of it is to make sure the jury members remember the important evidence and that they understand its relevance to your case.

After the summations, your trial is over, so the jury members head into the jury room with a copy of the jury instructions, all of the exhibits which have been admitted, and their notes if the judge has allowed them to take notes during the trial. They will take as much time as they need to review and discuss the evidence, apply it to the instructions from the judge, and, ultimately, make a decision. Once they have decided, they will inform the judge, who will call everybody back to the courtroom for the reading of the verdict.

After the verdict, the lawyers are allowed to speak to the jurors. I always take advantage of this opportunity to find out what factors impacted their decision and to learn what I could do better next time. The fact is, there's always room for improvement, and the lawyer who isn't working to improve probably isn't someone you want representing you.

Finally, the verdict is entered as a judgment, and your case is finished. Of course, it could be appealed, but the grounds for appeal are narrow, and they are usually denied. In order for an appeal to be granted, you must show some actual error at trial that resulted in prejudice to one of the parties. The bottom line is that once the verdict comes in and is entered as a judgment, your case is probably—finally—over. If you win, in most cases, you can expect to see your money within a few weeks.

CONCLUSION

As you can see, a real trial is nothing like the trials you see on television (unless you spend hours watching Court TV). Your lawyer should be able to explain each phase of the trial to you in advance so there are no surprises along the way. Hopefully, you will be able to resolve your claim without the need to go to trial, but if you can't, it's good to understand exactly what to expect at trial and what your lawyer is doing to prepare.

We have now covered all aspects of the personal injury claims process, from optimizing your insurance coverage all the way through the end of trial. The general principles we have explored apply to all personal injury claims, but every case is unique and your lawyer must be aware of the particular circumstances that make your case different. One of the most important differentiating factors is when the injured person is a child. In the final chapter, we will discuss concerns specific to claims involving injured children.

CHAPTER 22
DEALING WITH CLAIMS FOR CHILDREN

While we try to teach our children all about life,
our children teach us what life is all about.

— Angela Schwindt

While part of a lawyer's job is to give his clients a more objective, less emotional perspective on their claims, I often find myself angry about the injustice my clients have had to endure. It's bad enough that they were hurt by a careless driver or a negligent property owner, but they've often had to suffer the indignity of an indifferent or even hostile insurance company. If they need to litigate their claims, they will likely suffer through more aggressive tactics from insurance company lawyers, even though they have protection from their own attorneys. However, knowing what a claim is likely worth, I am able to set my emotion aside and help my clients make the right decisions for their families.

The biggest professional challenge I ever face is setting aside my emotional reaction when my client is an injured child. As adults, it is our responsibility to keep children safe. As a parent, I know how difficult that job can sometimes be. Children lack the sense and the experience to keep themselves out of harm's way. That's why I get so angry when the carelessness or indifference of adults results in injuries—sometimes serious injuries to children. One of the things I am most proud of is my consistent willingness to take on difficult cases involving injured children.

Every chapter in this book applies to all types of injury claims, from car wrecks to slips and falls and from dog bites to medical malpractice. Almost everything I have written applies to claims of adults as well as children. However, special considerations exist when making a claim on behalf of a child. Children often require different kinds of medical treatment than adults. Children can't sign for themselves so a lawyer must be hired by a parent or guardian on their behalf. Children can't consent to a settlement, so a procedure has been established to have an independent attorney, or *guardian ad litem*, review the settlement to insure it is in the child's best interest. Even with the *guardian ad litem's* approval, most children's settlements must be approved by a judge before the settlement can be made final. If the claim can't be settled, there are differences in the statute of limitations—the time the child has to file a lawsuit before the claim expires.

This chapter addresses some of the special circumstances and procedures that affect children's claims.

SPECIAL TREATMENT FOR KIDS

Following a car wreck or another injury, the treatment for children begins similarly to the treatment for adults. If an ambulance or paramedics arrive at the scene, then children should always be checked out at the scene, and if there is any question about whether they were injured, they should be taken to the emergency room and checked out as soon as possible after the injury. A follow-up visit with their pediatrician is always a good idea as well.

In the days and weeks following an injury to a child, the parents should pay careful attention to the child's behavior and take notes regarding any changes they observe. This is especially true for the youngest kids who can't always communicate with words what they are feeling. If any changes are noticed in a child's mood, appetite, sleep patterns, or behavior, they should definitely be checked out.

After these initial examinations, a typical course of action for an adult might include chiropractic, physical therapy, or other types of treatment. This is where the treatment for children definitely diverges from that of adults.

When my son Abraham was a newborn, he developed a common condition called plagiocephaly, or flat head syndrome. This condition results from a child sleeping in the same position every night and compressing a part of his soft skull, resulting in a flat spot. If left untreated, it can result in significant deformity of the child's head and face. Plagiocephaly is commonly treated by placing a helmet on the child's head for twenty-three hours a day for several months while the skull grows into the shape of the helmet, correcting the flat spot. We considered that treatment, but our pediatrician recommended that we first try a local pediatric chiropractor. Although I've been an injury attorney for many years, I had never heard of a chiropractor who only treats infants and children.

It turns out the chiropractic profession has a pediatric specialty just like medical doctors do. These chiropractors go through years of additional education and training to become certified as pediatric specialists. I have seen and been treated myself by many different chiropractors, but none of them worked the way I saw the pediatric chiropractor treat my son. After less than a month, the flat spot on his head was noticeably smaller, and after several months, it was basically resolved. While most chiropractors are willing and able to treat children and even infants, I have begun suggesting to the parents of children injured in car wrecks that they have their kids checked out by a certified pediatric chiropractor.

SPECIAL EXPERTS FOR KIDS

Claims for children often require expert witnesses we never see in adult cases. When choosing an attorney for your child's claim, it is important to find one with experience representing children and with knowledge of specialized experts that might be necessary.

Four-year-old Amanda Carp was playing in the playground of her preschool, which was located in a corner of a public park. After getting bored with the swings, she wandered out of the designated playground area to another part of the park with a few other kids and began running and jumping off a large cement structure onto hard-packed dirt. Just as she was about to make her next jump, she caught her foot on the edge of the structure and fell head first onto the dirt. Amanda sustained a severe concussion. Immediately after the fall, she lost consciousness and suffered a major seizure. Afterwards, she suffered from headaches and learning disabilities.

When Amanda's mom contacted me, I immediately considered several possible claims. First, when you entrust your child to other adults, whether in day care, preschool, or school, they have a duty to provide adequate supervision. Could better supervision in this case have prevented Amanda's injuries? Second, playgrounds must be designed and constructed with the safety of children in mind. Was the structure that Amanda fell from unreasonably dangerous? Should the designated playground area have been enclosed by a fence? These were all questions that had to be answered by an expert. Fortunately, I knew that in Seattle we have one of the foremost playground safety experts in the nation.

I contacted the expert and made an appointment to meet him at the scene of the injury. He surveyed the area, took photographs and measurements, and ultimately provided me with a report documenting the multiple ways in which the preschool violated safety standards. He also documented that the concrete structure was high enough to have required some kind of padded surface under it rather than hard-packed dirt. Finally, he stated that the preschool had a duty to keep its play area fenced in to prevent the kids from wandering off.

With this report in hand, we were able to persuade the insurance company to offer Amanda a very reasonable settlement for her injuries. Equally important, we were able to get the preschool to install a fence around its play area, and the City to redesign the park to be safer and more fun for kids. Without an expert witness who specializes in children's safety, such an outcome would not have been possible.

SPECIAL CLAIMS FOR KIDS

As I said in this chapter's introduction, kids often lack the good sense and experience to look out for their own safety. It is the responsibility of adults to protect children—sometimes from their own recklessness. This is the principle behind the claim of attractive nuisance. An attractive nuisance claim is based on the premise that some dangerous things can be so irresistible to kids that adults have a duty to block access, or at least make access difficult. Attractive nuisance claims can apply to abandoned cars, swimming pools, rooftops, and basically any dangerous condition on the property of a landowner where children may not be able to appreciate the risk of the condition.

Ten-year-old Billy Jackson walked home from school every day. His route took him past a house with a large trampoline in the front yard. One day, on his way home from school, Billy set down his book bag and climbed onto the trampoline. After jumping for a few minutes, he fell off and broke his leg.

Billy's dad came to me to see whether he had a claim. Although Billy was technically a trespasser, he was also a ten-year-old kid. Kids are simply not held to the same legal standard of care as adults, and rightfully so. Billy was unable to appreciate the danger from the trampoline, and he was unable to resist the temptation of seeing it there day after day. This was a clear case of attractive nuisance.

The homeowner's insurance company didn't even fight this one. Of course, we still had to prove the reasonable value of Billy's injuries, and we had to fight to get a fair recovery for his pain and suffering, but ultimately, we were able to get him a great recovery.

SPECIAL SETTLEMENT PROCEDURES FOR KIDS

Finally, after getting the appropriate medical treatment for your kids, hiring the right expert witnesses, and identifying the correct claims, your lawyer has negotiated a great settlement. Now you're done, right? Wrong. The law in Washington protects children from quick settlements that may not be in their best interests. This protection is done through a two-step process. First, an independent attorney or "guardian ad litem" (GAL) is appointed by the court. If a lawsuit hasn't already been filed, I usually need to file a petition to have a GAL appointed. The GAL reviews the medical records, interviews the parents and sometimes the injured child, reviews the proposed settlement for reasonableness, and makes a recommendation to the court. Then a judge will review the proposed settlement along with the GAL's report and make a final ruling approving or rejecting the settlement. Once the settlement is approved, the funds are generally required to be placed in a blocked, interest-bearing account until the child turns eighteen.

Of course, court fees are involved in getting a child's settlement approved, and the GAL has fees as well. I can usually get the insurance company to agree to pay these costs, but sometimes, I need to seek a court order forcing it to pay. Either way, I always work to maximize the net recovery to your child and to reduce any expenses that might need to be deducted from the settlement.

CONCLUSION

At their heart, claims for injuries to children are similar to claims made by adults, but several important differences have the potential to trip you up and complicate the claim. It is always a good idea with an injured child to consult a personal injury lawyer with specific experience handling claims for children. Doing so will help make sure your child gets the treatment she needs, and that the case is properly worked up to maximize her financial recovery from the insurance company.

PUTTING IT INTO ACTION

The best way out is always through.

— Robert Frost

Now that you've read this book, what are you going to do? You know that after you are injured in a car wreck or other incident, you have rights, but who will protect them? Who will have your back when the insurance companies are coming at you? Who will take care of the day-to-day hassles of your claim while you focus on healing your injuries and taking care of your family?

I challenge you to take action. Apply the lessons you've learned in this book to your situation. If you've already been injured, go back and make sure you've done everything right. Did you get all of the documentation you need? Do you know how to contact the witnesses? Did you get photos? If you haven't yet given a statement to the insurance company, tell it you won't be doing so until you speak to a lawyer, and then find the right lawyer for you using the questions in Chapter 9. If you haven't been in an accident, congratulations for having the foresight to educate yourself in advance. Now review your auto insurance to make sure you have the right coverage to protect your family and make sure every driver in your family knows what to do if he or she is ever in an auto accident.

Whether you've been injured or not, there are things you can do right now to help yourself and your family. In the lines below, list ten action items you will commit to doing over the next ninety days. Then do them. Don't delay.

1. _____
   _____

2. _____
   _____

3. _____
   _____

4. _____
   _____

5. _____
   _____

6. _____
   _____

7. _____
   _____

8. _____
   _____

9. _____
   _____

10. _____
    _____

In this book, you learned how to optimize your insurance coverage to make sure you are protected from liability, but also so you and your family are covered if you are hit by an uninsured or underinsured driver. You learned what to do and what not to do at the scene of an accident. You learned how to get the treatment you need after you are injured in an accident, and you learned the questions to ask when you are trying to choose the right lawyer. You learned how to recover the value of your damaged or totaled vehicle following a crash, and you learned how complications—even small complications—can jeopardize your case. You learned how insurance companies can make it difficult for you to recover fair value for your claim and how a lawyer can help you overcome these difficulties. You learned how a claim can be resolved through negotiation, mediation, arbitration, or trial. Finally, you learned a little bit about what a real trial looks like.

Now that you've read this book, I encourage you to contact me. Depending on the facts of your case and where your accident took place, I may or may not be able to represent you, but either way I'd love to hear from you. Tell me what you liked about this book, and what could be improved, but most importantly, tell me your story. Tell me how you overcame your injuries. Tell me how you dealt with the insurance company. Tell me how you made sure your injured child was fairly compensated for her injury and how you made sure nobody else's child would be hurt that way again. Tell me about your struggles and your challenges. I want to hear from you, and I want to help you if I can. My email address is matt@ dubinlawoffice.com. My phone number is 206-720-1501. Call me to schedule a phone conference or an in-person meeting. I would like to offer you a free, no-obligation legal consultation by phone, in person, or by Skype.

I wish you and your family nothing but the best on your journey.

I wish you health, happiness, and prosperity. If you've been hurt, I wish you a speedy and complete recovery, and I wish for you a successful outcome to your claim. You are the reason I wrote this book, and you are the reason I go to work every day. Be well. Be happy. And live a life filled with joy and purpose, fully understanding your rights and how to protect yourself and your family.

Matthew D. Dubin

APPENDICES

BICYCLE ACCIDENT FAQS

Can I sue the driver of a car that hits me while I'm riding my bicycle?

Yes. If the driver was at fault, you can make a claim for your injuries.

Is there anyone else I can make a claim against if I am injured in a bicycle accident?

Although the most common claim is against the driver who hit you, claims are possible for negligent design or manufacture of the bicycle, negligent service or maintenance on the vehicle that hit you, or even a claim against the city or government agency responsible for designing and maintaining the path or roadway you were riding on.

What damages can I recover in a bicycle accident case?

Just as with a car accident case, victims of a bicycle accident may recover the cost of their medical bills, lost earnings, and other expenses. In addition, a bicycle accident victim may make a recovery for pain, emotional distress, disability, disfigurement, loss of enjoyment of life, damage to family relationships, and impaired future earnings. In the case of a death caused by a bicycle accident, the family may receive compensation for the pain and suffering of their family member before his death, as well as loss of emotional support, love, affection, and care, and in certain cases, loss of economic support.

What if I was partly at fault for my bicycle accident?

Bicycles are subject to the same rules of the road as motor vehicles.

Additionally, bicyclists have a general duty to exercise reasonable care for the safety of themselves and others. However, even if you are partly at fault for your bicycle accident, you can still make a recovery for your injuries. Any damages you recover will be reduced by your percentage of fault. So if your damages are worth $100,000, but you were 40 percent at fault, you would still be entitled to recover $60,000.

What if my child was injured or killed while riding a bicycle?

Injuries to children are handled differently than other claims, and it is important that you consult with an attorney experienced in handling claims for injuries to children. Please see Chapter 22 for issues specific to claims involving injuries to children. If your child was injured while riding a bicycle, a claim could be made against the driver who caused the accident. If the accident results in a child's death, the family may have a wrongful death claim against the driver.

What if a pothole or other defect in the roadway caused my bicycle accident?

While an operator of a bicycle has a duty to pay attention, sometimes defects in the roadway, such as potholes, are so big or difficult to avoid that the city or other governmental entity may be responsible for the injury. However, there are many complicating factors in claims against governmental entities. If you believe you were injured as a result of a pothole or other road defect, you should contact an attorney immediately.

What if improper repairs or maintenance caused my bicycle accident?

If you brought your bicycle into a shop for repairs or maintenance shortly before your accident, and you believe the work was done improperly, you could have a claim against the person or shop that performed the repairs. However, you would need to prove the accident was caused by the negligence of the person who did the repairs. In cases like this, prompt investigation could mean the difference between making a recovery and having no case at all.

Do I need an expert witness for my bicycle accident case?

While not always necessary, an expert witness can be an important part of establishing liability in a bicycle accident case. Expert witnesses can determine the speed of the vehicles involved and express opinions on the most likely way the accident happened. They can also provide testimony regarding the rules of the road as applied to bicycles and motor vehicles.

Who will pay my medical bills following a bicycle accident?

Insurance coverage following a bicycle accident can get complicated. If the vehicle that hit you has personal injury protection (PIP) coverage, that coverage will pay your medical bills. If the driver did not have PIP coverage, then the bicyclist's own auto insurance or health insurance could provide coverage. An experienced bicycle accident attorney will work with all of the involved insurance companies to make sure the appropriate entity is paying your medical bills. Ultimately, any recovery made from the driver who caused the accident should include medical bills as well as non-economic damages.

How long do I have to file a lawsuit in a bicycle accident case?

All injury claims are subject to a statute of limitations, which requires that a lawsuit be filed within a certain time following the accident. Depending on the circumstances of the case, this period could vary. To determine the applicable statute of limitations in your state, you should consult with a personal injury attorney who is knowledgeable in bicycle accident cases as soon as possible following the accident.

Should I hire an attorney in my bicycle accident case?

It is important to have an experienced bicycle accident attorney to protect your rights and make sure the insurance company does not take advantage of you. An attorney can coordinate with all of the various insurance companies and health care providers, conduct a comprehensive investigation, and document your injuries to make sure you get the recovery you deserve.

CAR ACCIDENT FAQS

What should I do after a car accident?

The highest priority immediately following an accident is to stay safe. Leave the car where the accident occurred unless it is unsafe to do so. If you cannot leave your car where the accident happened, safely pull to the side of the road and remain in your car. Additional injuries can occur if proper precautions are not taken after an accident.

Whom should I call after a car accident?

Contact emergency personnel right away by calling 911. Even if there do not appear to be injuries that require immediate medical attention, you should still contact the police. The police will take statements and preserve evidence and witnesses. If the police refuse to come out because the accident was in a private parking lot or there were no injuries, gather the necessary information yourself before people leave the scene of the accident.

What information should I obtain following a car accident?

Collect the following information:

- As much detailed contact information as you can for the other drivers involved in the accident (name, address, phone numbers, email)

- Vehicle information for all vehicles involved in the accident (make, model, year, license plate number)

- Names and contact information for all passengers and witnesses at the scene of the accident

- Insurance information for all vehicles/drivers involved in the accident, including company name, policy number, and dates of coverage

- If police show up, you should also get the name, badge number, and department name for the investigating officer(s)

Should I talk to the police following a car accident?

Yes. You should fully cooperate with the police, explaining how the accident happened. You should not take fault for the accident, even if you think you have some share of the blame. Fault can be determined and apportioned later.

Should I take pictures at the scene of the accident?

Absolutely. These days, nearly everyone has a phone with a camera. You should photograph the damage to all involved vehicles, the overall accident scene, and any visible injuries. Take as many pictures as you can from many different angles. In car accidents, a picture is often worth a thousand words.

Should I seek medical attention following a car accident?

You should always seek medical attention after being involved in a car accident, even if you don't think you are hurt. Often a person experiences an adrenaline rush following a car accident. He is confused and disoriented and concerned about his family or, perhaps, his car. Sometimes a person is hurt but doesn't begin to experience symptoms until the next day, or even several days later. It is always best to be safe by getting checked out at a local emergency room or by your physician. Waiting too long to get checked out by a doctor could hurt your chances of making a fair recovery for your claim.

Should I call my insurance company?

It is not necessary to call your insurance company from the scene of the accident, but many insurance companies do require that you report an accident promptly. If you do call the insurance company before consulting with an attorney, you should only give the basic information about how the accident happened. If the company wants more details or if it wants to record your call, you should meet with an attorney before going any further.

Should I speak with the other driver's insurance company?

You should never speak to the other driver's insurance company on your own. Its employees are highly trained to find ways to pay you less than you deserve on your claim. You also have no obligation to speak to the other driver's insurance in order to make a claim for injuries or damage. You should always consult with a qualified car accident attorney before attempting to speak with the other driver's insurance company. If you say the wrong thing, it could prevent you from getting a full recovery, or any recovery, for your valid claim.

When should I contact an attorney following a car accident?

It's a good idea to contact a personal injury lawyer as soon as possible after you've been involved in a car accident. At the Law Offices of Matthew D. Dubin, an attorney will talk to you, with no charge or obligation, about the facts of your case, and determine whether a claim can be asserted. If you decide to hire us, we will coordinate all communications between insurance companies, health care providers, and other interested parties. We are dedicated to protecting the rights of our clients and preserving their personal injury claims.

COMMERCIAL TRUCK ACCIDENT FAQS

How is a commercial truck accident different from a car accident?

Most commercial trucks are required to carry higher levels of insurance. That means truck accident cases may be much bigger than the typical car accident case. Truck drivers are also subject to regulations that don't apply to drivers of private vehicles. Drivers are subject to limits on the hours they can drive, and they are required to keep a log of their hours. Trucking companies are required to perform background checks on their drivers, and they must perform periodic re-evaluations. Drivers are also subject to testing for drugs and alcohol.

What should I do immediately after being involved in a truck accident?

If you are involved in an accident with a commercial truck, you should follow the same steps outlined in our car accident FAQs: Call the police, gather information, take photographs, and seek medical attention. Do not speak to the truck's insurance company before consulting with a qualified truck accident attorney.

What kind of investigation is necessary in a truck accident case?

An experienced truck accident lawyer will immediately take steps to obtain the truck driver's log to make sure it was properly kept and the driver was observing limitations on driving hours when the accident took place. It is also important to obtain information regarding the vehicle's maintenance history and the driver's driving record. This information can be challenging to discover if not obtained right away, and the information discovered could be essential to getting you a full recovery for your injuries.

Is an expert witness necessary in a truck accident case?

Expert witnesses can be helpful in nearly every case, but they are especially important in truck accident cases. An expert witness can establish violations in safety inspections and driving logs. An expert witness can also help establish how the accident happened in cases where the trucking company is disputing liability.

What kinds of damages can I recover in a truck accident case?

Just as with a car accident case, victims of a truck accident may recover the cost of their medical bills, lost earnings, and other expenses. In addition, a truck accident victim may make a recovery for pain, emotional distress, disability, disfigurement, loss of enjoyment of life, damage to family relationships, and impaired future earnings. In the case of a death caused by a truck accident, the family may recover for the pain and suffering of their family member before his death, as well as loss of emotional support, love, affection, and care, and in certain cases, loss of economic support.

How long do I have to file a lawsuit in a trucking case?

All injury claims are subject to a statute of limitations, which requires that a lawsuit be filed within a certain time following the accident. Depending on the circumstances of the case, this period could vary. To determine the applicable statute of limitations in your state, you should consult with a personal injury attorney who is knowledgeable in truck accident cases as soon as possible following the accident.

Should I hire an attorney in my truck accident case?

Truck accident cases can be difficult and complicated. If certain steps aren't taken right away, your ability to make a full recovery for your loss may be compromised. Hiring an attorney early in the process will help you make sure that all of the proper information is obtained and your rights are protected. When you do hire an attorney, make sure he or she has experience handling truck cases and knows how these cases differ from car accident cases. Hiring an experienced truck accident lawyer, like those at the Law Offices of Matthew D. Dubin, will provide you with the peace of mind that every necessary step is being taken to protect you and your family.

DISC HERNIATION FAQS

What is a herniated disc?

The bones that form the spine in your neck and back are cushioned by small, spongy discs. When these discs are healthy, they act as shock absorbers for the spine and keep the spine flexible. But when a disc is damaged, it can bulge or even break open. This is called a herniated disc. It can also be called a slipped or ruptured disc. When a herniated disc bulges out from between the vertebrae, the spinal nerves and spinal cord can become pinched or compressed.

What is the cause of a herniated disc?

While a herniated disc could be caused by wear and tear as you age and the disc dries out, the most common cause of disc herniation is traumatic injury to the spine. Trauma can cause tears in the outer layer of the disc, allowing the gel inside the disc to be pushed out. This can cause the disc to bulge, break open, or even break into pieces.

What are the symptoms of a herniated disc?

When a herniated disc irritates the adjacent nerve, it can interfere with the pathway by which signals are sent from your brain to your extremities. A herniated disc can cause pain, numbness, and weakness in the affected area. A herniated disc in the lower back can cause pain and numbness in the buttock and down the leg. This is known as sciatica. Occasionally, a herniated disc can result in bowel or bladder problems. These symptoms could be a sign of a serious medical emergency and *you should see your doctor immediately if you have problems urinating, you have trouble having bowel movements, or you have numbness around your genitals.*

How is a herniated disc diagnosed?

A physician will often make a diagnosis of herniated disc based on a physical examination, but the most common basis for this diagnosis is an MRI or other imaging that shows the condition of the disc and its proximity to the affected nerve.

How is a herniated disc treated?

Physicians most commonly prefer to treat herniated discs conservatively at first, and they progress to more aggressive interventions only if the symptoms do not improve. Often, a doctor will order rest and avoidance of aggravating activities. Sometimes that is all it will take for the symptoms to resolve, but often the symptoms persist even with rest. Doctors also usually prescribe the use of heat and cold to relax the muscles in the back and relieve muscle spasms. If the symptoms don't improve, a doctor may order physical therapy and pain medications.

If none of these treatments provide relief, a physician can administer epidural steroid injections. These are injections of cortisone directly into the area of nerve compression. These treatments often reduce inflammation and relieve the compression of the nerve. Sometimes, these treatments will permanently resolve the symptoms.

If there is significant neurological deficit, or if the symptoms persist after all of the above treatments have been exhausted, surgery may be the only remaining option. Surgery can remove the entire disc or just the portion that is bulging in order to relieve the compression of the affected nerve.

Can I make a claim for my herniated disc injury?

Yes. If the injury was caused by a collision that was someone else's fault, you should be able to obtain full compensation for your medical bills, lost earnings, physical pain, emotional distress, and the impact on the quality of your life.

How long do I have to file a lawsuit in a herniated disc case?

All injury claims are subject to a statute of limitations, which requires that a lawsuit be filed within a certain time following the accident. Depending on the circumstances of the case, this period could vary. To determine the applicable statute of limitations in your state, you should consult with a personal injury attorney who is knowledgeable in herniated disc cases as soon as possible following the accident.

Should I hire an attorney in my herniated disc case?

It is essential that you consult with a qualified attorney before speaking to the other driver's insurance company. A herniated disc can be a complicated injury, and insurance companies will often try to claim that your injury was pre-existing and not caused by the accident. Other times, they will question the reasonableness of the treatment you received. Insurance companies have doctors available to them who commonly testify that your claims are exaggerated and your treatment was excessive and unreasonable. An attorney with experience handling herniated disc cases can prepare your case to overcome these objections by the insurance company to get you the best possible result.

MOTORCYCLE ACCIDENT FAQS

How many people are killed each year in motorcycle accidents?

Over 4,000 people die each year in motorcycle accidents. The most common cause for motorcycle fatalities is head injury. Although helmets decrease the chances for one, head injuries still happen frequently. Compared to car accidents, motorcyclists are thirty-seven times more likely to die in an accident each year. Even those motorcyclists who survive their accidents tend to suffer much more catastrophic injuries than those suffered by victims of car accidents.

What if I am involved in an accident that was not my fault?

Motorcycles face a much higher risk than cars of being hit by another vehicle. Motorcycles can be hard to see because of their size, especially for drivers of larger vehicles. Numerous situations can result in an accident that is not your fault. If you are involved in a motorcycle accident, you should follow the same steps outlined in our car accident FAQs: Call the police, gather information, take photographs, and seek medical attention. Do not speak to the other driver's insurance company before consulting with a qualified motorcycle accident attorney.

Who can sue for a motorcycle accident case?

Anyone injured in the accident can bring a claim—either the motorcycle operator or the passenger. If the operator was killed in the accident, certain family members are authorized to bring a survival or wrongful death claim under Washington law. The right to make such a claim can vary from state to state, and to be sure of your rights, you should consult a qualified motorcycle accident attorney in your state.

Who can be held responsible for injuries or death resulting from a motorcycle accident?

Whoever was at fault for causing the accident can be held responsible. Usually, it is the driver of a car or truck who caused the accident, but if the motorcycle operator is at fault for causing the accident, his passenger may have a claim against him. Although the claim is against the driver or operator who caused the accident, in almost every case, there is insurance that will provide coverage for the loss.

What kind of investigation is necessary in a motorcycle case?

As with any accident, a prompt investigation can be the difference between winning and losing. The insurance company will likely try to claim that the motorcycle operator was partially or completely at fault for causing the accident. An early investigation to identify witnesses, obtain physical evidence, and establish how the accident really happened is essential in every motorcycle case. An experienced motorcycle accident attorney will know exactly what kind of investigation needs to take place, and he will get the necessary information right away.

Is an expert witness necessary in a motorcycle accident case?

While not always necessary, an expert witness can be an important part of establishing a motorcycle accident case. Expert witnesses can determine the speed of the vehicles involved and can express opinions on the most likely way the accident happened. They can also provide testimony regarding the rules of the road as applied to motorcycles.

What kinds of damages can I recover in a motorcycle accident case?

Just as with victims of a car accident, victims of a motorcycle ac-

252

cident may recover the cost of their medical bills, lost earnings, and other expenses. In addition, a motorcycle accident victim may make a financial recovery for pain, emotional distress, disability, disfigurement, loss of enjoyment of life, damage to family relationships, and impaired future earnings. In the case of a death caused by a motorcycle accident, the family may recover compensation for the pain and suffering of their family member before his death, as well as loss of emotional support, love, affection, and care, and in certain cases, loss of economic support.

I don't have insurance on my motorcycle. Can I still make a claim for my injuries?

Absolutely. The fact that you did not have insurance on your motorcycle does not in any way prevent you from making a claim against the driver who caused the accident.

What if I was partly at fault for causing the motorcycle accident?

Even if you were partly at fault for causing the accident, you still may be entitled to make a recovery for your injuries. Under Washington law, which uses comparative negligence, your recovery will be reduced by your percentage of fault. So if you were 30 percent at fault for the accident and your case is worth $100,000, you may only recover $70,000. Other jurisdictions may have different ways of apportioning fault. To be sure of your rights, it's always a good idea to consult with a motorcycle accident attorney who practices where the accident took place.

How long do I have to file a lawsuit in a motorcycle case?

All injury claims are subject to a statute of limitations, which requires that a lawsuit be filed within a certain time following the accident. Depending on the circumstances of the case, this period could vary. To determine the applicable statute of limitations in your state, you should consult with a personal injury attorney who is knowledgeable in motorcycle accident cases as soon as possible following the accident.

Should I hire an attorney in my motorcycle accident case?

It is important to have an experienced motorcycle accident attorney to protect your rights and to make sure you are not abused by the insurance company. An attorney can coordinate with all of the various insurance companies and health care providers, can conduct a comprehensive investigation, and can document your injuries to make sure you get the recovery you deserve.

PEDESTRIAN ACCIDENTS FAQS

What should I do immediately after being involved in a pedestrian accident?

Above all, please make sure you are physically okay. If you think you might be hurt, stay where you are and wait for medical personnel to assist you. If you are hurt and you try to move around, you could injure yourself more seriously. Pedestrians who have been hit by motor vehicles are much more likely to be killed or seriously injured than occupants of cars. Once you have established that you are okay, if you are able, you should follow the same steps outlined in our car accident FAQs: Call the police, gather information, take photographs, and seek medical attention. Do not speak to the driver's insurance company before speaking with a qualified pedestrian accident attorney.

Can I make a claim against the driver who hit me?

Yes. As long as it can be shown that the driver was at least partly at fault for causing the accident, you can make a recovery for medical bills, lost earnings, and non-economic damages.

What if I was not walking in a crosswalk at the time of the accident?

It is always recommended that pedestrians obey the rules of the road and only cross at designated areas. However, just because you were not in the crosswalk does not mean you can't make a financial recovery for your injuries. Drivers have a duty under Washington law to exercise reasonable care for the safety of others sharing the road. Even if you are partially at fault for causing the accident, you can still make a recovery; however, any damages you recover will be reduced by your percentage of fault. This rule may vary from state to state, and to be sure of your rights, you should consult with an attorney in the state where the accident took place.

If I am a pedestrian hit by a motor vehicle, can I sue anyone other than the driver?

A qualified pedestrian accident attorney will explore every possible claim for damages you might have following an accident. For example, if the roadway or sidewalk was poorly designed or poorly lit, it could result in a claim against the city or other governmental entity responsible for the sidewalk. If there was recent maintenance on the vehicle that was done improperly, there may be a claim against the repair shop.

What kind of investigation is necessary in a pedestrian accident case?

As with any injury claim, a proper investigation could mean the difference between making a full recovery and not getting anything at all. An experienced pedestrian accident lawyer will determine the identities of the witnesses, get the maintenance history for the motor vehicle involved, and may even hire an accident reconstructionist to express an opinion about how the accident most likely happened.

Who will pay my medical bills following a pedestrian accident?

Insurance coverage following a pedestrian accident can get complicated. If the vehicle that hit you has personal injury protection (PIP) coverage, that coverage will pay your medical bills. If the driver did not have PIP coverage, then the pedestrian's own auto insurance or health insurance could provide coverage. Ultimately, any recovery made from the driver who caused the accident should include medical bills as well as non-economic damages.

What kind of damages can I recover in a pedestrian accident case?

Just as with a car accident case, victims of pedestrian accidents may recover the cost of their medical bills, lost earnings, and other expenses. In addition, a pedestrian accident victim may make a recovery for pain, emotional distress, disability, disfigurement, loss of enjoyment of life, damage to family relationships, and impaired future earnings. In the case of a death caused by a pedestrian accident, the family may recover compensation for the pain and suffering of their family member before his death, as well as loss of emotional support, love, affection, and care, and in certain cases, loss of economic support.

How long do I have to file a lawsuit in a pedestrian accident case?

All injury claims are subject to a statute of limitations, which requires that a lawsuit be filed within a certain time following the accident. Depending on the circumstances of the case, this period could vary. To determine the applicable statute of limitations in your state, you should consult with a personal injury attorney who is knowledgeable in pedestrian accident cases as soon as possible following the accident.

Should I hire an attorney in my pedestrian accident case?

It is important to have an experienced pedestrian accident attorney to protect your rights and make sure the insurance company does not take advantage of you. An attorney can coordinate with all of the various insurance companies and health care providers, can conduct a comprehensive investigation, and can document your injuries to make sure you get the recovery you deserve.

GLOSSARY OF USEFUL TERMS

AAJ – The American Association for Justice (formerly known as the Association of Trial Lawyers of America) is a national organization of lawyers who represent accident victims.

Accident – An occurrence caused by someone's negligence.

Accident Reconstructionist – An individual employed to conduct in-depth collision analysis and reconstruction to identify the collision causation and contributing factors in different types of collisions, including the role of the driver(s), vehicle(s), roadway, and the environment.

Affidavit – A sworn written statement signed under the penalty of perjury, in the presence of a notary public.

Adjuster – A representative of an insurance company whose job it is to settle a claim made under an insurance policy.

Alternative Dispute Resolution ("ADR") – Procedures for settling disputes by means other than litigation, such as by arbitration, mediation, or minitrials. Such procedures, which are usually less costly and less time consuming than litigation, are increasingly being used to resolve motor vehicle claims.

Appeal – A request that a higher court review the findings of a lower court.

Arbitration – An informal proceeding used to save time and money in an attempt to resolve disputes in place of a trial before a judge or jury.

At Fault Driver – The negligent driver who caused an accident.

Attorney – An individual who has completed four years of under-graduate studies and three additional years of an American Bar Association-approved law school, passed the bar exam, and was found to be fit to practice law by the Supreme Court of a particular state.

Attractive Nuisance – A legal doctrine that places a duty upon landowners to take steps to prevent injury to children from a potentially dangerous condition on their properties which might attract children to come and play.

Bodily Injury Liability – Insurance coverage that pays claims to a person for injuries caused by another driver's negligence.

Carrier – An insurance company.

Case in Chief – The portion of a trial during which the plaintiff presents evidence in support of his position.

Civil Action – A lawsuit brought for money damages.

Claim – The assertion of a right; a demand for payment in accordance with an insurance policy or a demand for something as rightful or due another.

Collision Coverage – Under this type of automobile coverage, your own insurance company will pay for any property damage to your car subject to a deductible. Collision coverage is generally subject to a deductible.

Comparative Negligence – Any negligent act or conduct on the part of the person making a claim that may have contributed to the accident.

Complaint – The first pleading filed with the clerk of the court by a plaintiff setting forth his or her allegations against a specific person or entity including theories of negligence.

Comprehensive Coverage – A type of first-party auto insurance that covers theft, fire, vandalism, weather damage, and other similar circumstances that may cause damage to a vehicle. Comprehensive auto insurance does not usually cover acts of God, theft or vandalism by family members or employees, contents of the vehicle, tires, or damage due to improper maintenance.

Contingent Fee – A fee charged for a lawyer's services only if the lawsuit is successful or is favorably settled out of court.

Damages – The physical and financial losses suffered by a plaintiff.

Decedent – A dead or deceased person.

Defendant – The person who is being sued in a lawsuit.

Defense Counsel – The attorneys who are hired (usually by the insurance company) to represent a defendant.

Demand Package – Formal letter from an attorney on behalf of a client, demanding payment or some other action from another party. Although commonly not a legal necessity in filing a suit, a demand letter is sent usually to settle the matter without litigation or to put pressure on the other party.

Deposition – An out-of-court sworn oral statement of a party or a witness in connection with a lawsuit, which is transcribed by a court reporter.

Discovery – A period of time after the filing of a lawsuit, during which the parties can investigate facts through interrogatories, depositions, document requests, and subpoenas.

Eggshell Plaintiff – A legal concept that requires the defendant to take the victim as he finds him. If the victim is more susceptible to injury than an average individual would be, the defendant is still liable for all the damages that occur, even if he would have had to pay much less had he injured someone else.

ERISA – Benefits paid to an employee as part of a qualified employer-sponsored benefit program under the Employee Retirement Income Security Act of 1974. Benefits paid under a qualified ERISA plan may be exempt from Washington insurance law.

Essential Services Coverage – A type of benefit that is part of Washington's Personal Injury Protection (PIP), reimbursing the cost of needed household and domestic help following an injury.

Expert Witness – An individual hired in connection with a lawsuit to provide factual and opinion testimony in connection with a topic outside the normal knowledge of a juror.

Federal Court – Courts created by an Act of Congress to prosecute federal crimes and resolve civil disputes against the federal government, constitutional claims, and disputes between citizens of different states.

Filing – The physical act of delivering to the clerk of a court a pleading or document for the court's consideration.

Filing Fee – The sum of money required to be paid to the clerk of the court before a document can be accepted by the clerk and deemed ready to be filed.

First-Party Claim – A claim brought against one's own insurance carrier or against a carrier obligated by law or contract to pay a claim, such as a workers' compensation or PIP insurance carrier.

GAP Insurance – A type of property damage insurance that in the event of the total loss of a vehicle will pay the difference between the vehicle's actual cash value and the current outstanding balance on any loan or lease.

Guardian Ad Litem – An independent attorney appointed by the court to represent the interests of a child or an otherwise incapacitated person.

IME ("Independent Medical Examination") – Although called independent, such an examination should properly be called an insurance medical examination or a defense medical examination. It is a medical examination at the request of the insurance company or its attorney that is usually biased in favor of the insurance company.

Insurance – A contract in which an individual or entity pays money in advance to another to receive financial protection or reimbursement for unforeseen losses or claims.

Interrogatories – Written questions that are part of the discovery process, to be answered under oath and in writing as required under the Washington Court Rules.

Jury Instructions – The directive given by the judge to a jury prior to deliberations as to what laws apply to the facts of the case.

Judgment – A decision or order signed by a judge that determines the rights and obligations of the litigants. A jury verdict is enforceable and collectable only after a judge "enters judgment."

Letter of Protection (Also known as Letter of Guarantee) – A letter from an attorney to a health care provider guaranteeing that upon resolution of the case through negotiation or litigation, the provider will be paid in full before any funds are released to the client. This document creates a contractual relationship between the attorney and the health care provider, and an attorney should only sign such a document with the permission of the client.

Lien – An outstanding sum of money that attaches to a case and must be paid out of the final settlement proceeds.

Litigation – A legal action, or lawsuit, including all of the proceedings that take place after a lawsuit is filed.

Loss of Consortium – A claim belonging to the spouse of an injured person for damage to the marital relationship, including loss of material services, society, guidance, companionship, and sexual relations.

Mediation – A private, informal dispute resolution process in which a neutral third person, the mediator, helps disputing parties to reach an agreement. The mediator has no power to impose a decision on the parties.

Mitigation of Damages – A duty imposed upon an injured person to attempt to minimize his damages, or avoid aggravating the injury. Failure to mitigate your damages could result in a reduced financial recovery.

Motion – A pleading filed with the court seeking a specified ruling or court order most commonly used to compel opposing counsel to provide discovery.

Motion in Limine – A pretrial motion asking the court to prohibit opposing counsel from referring to evidence on matters that are irrelevant, inadmissible or highly prejudicial.

MRI (Magnetic Resonance Imaging) – A type of imaging machine using magnetic force to produce internal soft tissue images that are interpreted by a radiologist.

NADA (National Automobile Dealers Association) – A service used by insurance companies to value used automobiles.

Narrative Report – A report prepared by a treating or non-treating doctor who has been hired as an expert witness for a fee, which discusses a person's injuries, the cause of such injuries, as well as the permanency of those injuries.

Negligence – The failure to exercise the standard of care that a reasonably prudent person would have exercised under the same or similar circumstances.

Negotiation – The process of making offers and counteroffers until an acceptable offer is made and accepted.

Objective Tests – Objective medical tests, such as MRI, X-ray, or CT scans, that are not based on the person's voluntary responses, such as pain. Objective medical tests cannot be faked or exaggerated.

Parties – The litigants involved in a lawsuit.

Personal Injury Protection – Known as "PIP" benefits, these first-party insurance benefits are payable to a person injured in a motor vehicle accident. Benefits usually include medical bill payment, income continuation benefits, funeral benefits, and essential services payable regardless of fault.

PIP – See Personal Injury Protection above.

PIP Suit – A legal proceeding, usually in the form of an arbitration, against an automobile insurance carrier to force it to pay justified PIP insurance benefits.

Plaintiff – A person who brings a case against another in a court of law.

Pleading – A formal, written statement filed with the court by a party in a civil action, such as a complaint or an answer.

Premises Liability – An accident that occurred due to a landowner or storekeeper's negligence.

Preponderance of Evidence – The standard of proof required in a civil trial that proves a fact or event "more likely than not."

Pro Se – An individual representing himself or herself before a court without a lawyer.

Property Damage Liability – Insurance coverage that pays for physical damage to another person's property or motor vehicle that was caused by the policyholder's negligence.

Rebuttal – Evidence introduced to counter, disprove, or contradict the opposition's evidence or a presumption, or responsive legal argument.

Redirect Examination – Further examination of a witness after cross-examination, carried out by the party that first called the witness.

Retainer Agreement – A written agreement that hires an attorney's services and sets forth how the attorney will be paid.

Release – A written document that, when signed, discharges a person or entity from any further legal responsibility or liability.

Reserve – The amount of money an insurance company sets aside in anticipation of paying a claim.

Rest – In a lawsuit, a party is said to "rest," or "rest her case," when that party indicates that she has produced all the evidence that she intends to offer at that stage and submits the case either finally, or subject to the right to offer rebutting evidence after her opponent has introduced her evidence.

Serve – To make legal delivery of a document, pleading, notice, summons, complaint, or subpoena upon another person or entity in the fashion and format prescribed by the rules of court.

Settlement – An agreement between the parties to end a legal dispute or lawsuit.

Settlement Conference – A conference held before a judge to narrow the differences between the parties in hope of reaching a settlement.

Soft Tissue – Body parts other than bone, such as nerves, muscles, blood vessels, and the brain.

Statute of Limitations – A law that establishes a time limit for suing in a civil case.

Strict Liability – Liability that does not depend upon the actual negligence or intent of another but is based upon a breach of a duty to make something or some situation absolutely safe.

Structured Settlement – A tax-free settlement that will be paid in future periodic payments.

Subpoena – A legal document that compels a person or corporation to appear at a designated time and place, for the purpose of giving testimony or producing documents.

Subrogation – A legal right of one who has paid an obligation that another should have paid, to be paid back by the other. When a first-party coverage such as PIP pays your accident-related medical bills, your insurance company has a right to subrogation from your third-party recovery.

Summary Judgment – A procedural device used during civil litigation to dispose of a case promptly and expeditiously without a trial. It is used when there is no dispute as to the material facts of the case and a party is entitled to judgment as a Matter of Law.

Summation – A lawyer's closing arguments at the conclusion of a trial.

Summons – A legal notice requiring a person to appear in court or answer a lawsuit.

Survival Action – A lawsuit brought by a deceased person's estate for injuries or damages suffered by the deceased between the time of the injury and the person's death.

Third-Party Lawsuit – A claim brought against an insurance carrier other than your own. Although in Washington a lawsuit must be against the negligent individual, the reality is that his or her insurance company provides a defense attorney and pays any award made against that individual.

Torts – A civil wrong arising out of a breach of a duty or act of negligence for which an injured party is entitled to an award of damages.

Tort Reform – A movement to reduce the amount of tort litigation by passing anti-consumer laws to restrict or take away the rights of individuals to access the courts for awards of damages.

Trial de Novo – A new trial ordered on the entire case usually resulting from an appeal of an unfavorable arbitration award.

Underinsured Motorist Coverage (UIM) – Insurance coverage that pays for losses and injuries caused by a negligent driver who lacks sufficient insurance coverage to cover the damages.

Uninsured Motorist Coverage (UM) – Insurance coverage that pays for losses and injuries caused by a negligent driver who was uninsured at the time of an accident.

Venue – The county having jurisdiction or location of a legal forum where a trial on a particular matter will occur.

Verdict – The final findings of a jury regarding questions of fact and damages after applying the law as read to it by the judge.

Voir Dire – The pretrial interview conducted by the court or by the attorneys for the parties to evaluate potential jurors' fairness, fitness, and impartiality prior to being selected as jurors.

Workers' Compensation – A system for providing benefits to workers who are injured on the job, regardless of fault.

WSAJ – The Washington State Association for Justice (formerly the Washington State Trial Lawyers Association).

Wrongful Death Claim – A lawsuit on behalf of a deceased person's survivors for the future economic losses they will suffer; it is brought against the negligent party who caused the death.

ABOUT THE AUTHOR

Matthew D. Dubin has practiced law in Washington since 1995. During the past twenty years, he has helped thousands of people and families affected by almost every type of personal injury claim imaginable.

Matt attended Yale University, where in 1990 he received his Bachelor of Arts Degree in History. After working briefly for the law firm of Boyle, Vogeler, & Haimes in New York City, he moved to Seattle and enrolled in law school. Three years later, he received his Juris Doctor degree from the University of Washington. In 1995, he was admitted to the Washington Bar and began his law practice.

Matt is the founder of the Law Offices of Matthew D. Dubin. His main concentration includes all areas of personal injury law. Although most of his cases are resolved prior to trial, Matt has always believed that the only way an insurance company will pay fair compensation for a claim is if it sees that the plaintiff is ready to try the case to a jury.

Matt has consistently given back to the legal community by being an active member of the American Association for Justice and the Washington State Association for Justice (WSAJ), in which he has been an Eagle member since 2011.

Matt has published articles on topics including dog bite law, distracted driving, traffic fatalities, bicycle safety, dangerous household products, traumatic brain injuries, health insurance, pedestrian safety, risks facing teenage drivers, and more.

On the personal side, Matt has been a tenor with the Seattle Symphony Chorale, the official choral group of the Seattle Symphony, since 2000. He is a coach with the North Seattle Baseball Association, and he is a member of the Haller Lake Community Club in North Seattle. He enjoys hiking, camping, and attending sporting events with his wife Elizabeth and his son Abraham.

Professional Associations and Ratings

Washington State Bar Association (WSBA)

King County Bar Association (KCBA)

American Association for Justice (AAJ)

Washington State Association for Justice (WSAJ)

The National Motor Vehicle Trial Lawyers Association

The National Trial Lawyers (Top 100 Trial Lawyers)

The National Association of Personal Injury Attorneys (Top 10 Attorneys)

The American Society of Legal Advocates (ASLA) (Top 100 Lawyers)

The National Association of Distinguished Counsel (Top One Percent Attorney)

AVVO.com (10.0 – Superb)

Martindale-Hubbell (AV – Preeminent for Ethical Standards and Legal Ability)

Areas of Expertise

Civil Jury Trials

Personal Injury and Wrongful Death Cases

Catastrophic Injury Cases

Injuries to Children

Motor Vehicle Accidents

Automobile Accidents

Motorcycle and Bicycle Accidents

Pedestrian Accidents

Truck and Eighteen-Wheeler Accidents

Premises Liability and Slip, Trip, and Fall Cases

Ice and Snow-Related Accidents

Supermarket and Store Accidents

Spinal Injury Cases

Traumatic Brain Injury Cases

Medical, Nursing, and Legal Malpractice Cases

Animal Attacks and Dog Bite Cases

Machine and Defective Product Cases

Inadequate Security Cases

Mass Transit and Taxi Cases

Ride Share Cases

ABOUT THE LAW OFFICES OF MATTHEW D. DUBIN

Welcome to the Law Offices of Matthew D. Dubin. We hope this is the start of a fruitful relationship. It is important to us that our clients feel their needs are understood and honored. We work for you and will go to any lengths on your behalf in aggressively pursuing your goals.

Helping clients pursue compensation in car accidents and other personal injury cases has been the exclusive focus of our law firm since 1998. You deal with your attorney personally, and you can always reach your lawyer when you need to talk.

Based in Seattle, Washington, our firm handles a full spectrum of personal injury claims for clients in Bellevue, Everett, Tacoma, and all surrounding communities in King, Snohomish, and Pierce counties, and throughout the State of Washington. If you were injured in a motor vehicle accident, a slip and fall, or by medical or dental malpractice, we are happy to evaluate your potential claim in a free consultation.

It's About What You Want

We try to understand each client's individual needs. With a combined twenty-five years of experience, we know it's not necessarily about getting the most money. You may prefer a smaller settlement sooner. You may want justice against a wrongdoer. You may be concerned about getting the best medical care for your family member. We take the time to listen, then follow your wishes.

As Aggressive As Necessary

The Law Offices of Matthew D. Dubin is prepared to do what it takes to achieve your goals. We ask for no more than what you rightfully deserve for the financial and personal impact on your life—but certainly no less. We prefer to be cooperative and settlement-minded in negotiations, but we are as aggressive as the insurance company requires us to be. We strive to be compassionate and approachable to clients, but we are fierce adversaries when dealing with those who stand in the way of our clients' recovery.

If we agree to take your case, it's because we believe it has a strong legal basis. That fact, combined with the attention and expertise that we exercise in moving your case forward, almost always result in a favorable outcome. Sometimes the law is not squarely on your side or the insurance limits are too low to collect full damages. Yet by thoroughly preparing claims and consulting the best experts, we maximize your chances of obtaining a fair recovery, whether your case involves a car accident, professional malpractice, or some other personal injury.

Free Case Evaluation • No Recovery, No Fee

At the Law Offices of Matthew D. Dubin, we collect no attorneys' fees unless we secure compensation on your behalf. This means that you do not need to worry about out-of-pocket expenses for attorneys' fees.

Talk to us if you wonder whether you have a viable claim, and let us take care of your legal worries. We aggressively pursue your full damages, and we are here to help when the other party's insurance won't pay your doctors, or your own insurer gives you the run-around. Contact us directly at 206-720-1501. We often visit injured clients at their homes or in the hospital.

www.DubinLawOffice.com

LAW OFFICES OF
MATTHEW D. DUBIN

LAW OFFICES OF
MATTHEW D. DUBIN

Washington State Personal Injury Attorneys

What to Do If You Are in a Car (or Other Motor Vehicle) Accident

How to use this form

Even if your accident was completely someone else's fault, you can severely impair your ability to make a full recovery for your injuries by making some simple and common mistakes at the scene of the collision. This form is designed to walk you step-by-step through what you need to do after being involved in a motor vehicle accident. We intentionally kept it simple so even if you are in shock, you should be able to follow these instructions and preserve your claim. If you have any questions about anything in this form, please call us to clarify BEFORE you are in an accident. We'd be happy to hear from you.

Stay safe at the accident scene

Leave the car where the accident occurred, unless it is unsafe to do so. This will allow the police to document properly and accurately the facts of the accident. If you cannot leave your car at the collision scene, pull safely to the side of the road and remain in your vehicle. Additional injuries can occur if proper precautions are not taken after the accident.

Call the police

Contact emergency personnel right away after an accident. The police will take statements from parties to the accident and will preserve evidence and witnesses. If the police refuse to come to the scene because the accident was in a private parking lot or there were no apparent injuries, get the other driver's insurance information, address, and phone number, as well as contact information for any witnesses. If possible, take a picture of the other driver's license and insurance card. Use this page to record all the information you obtain.

Take as many pictures as you can

These days nearly everyone has a phone with a camera. You should photograph the damage to vehicles, the overall scene, and any visible injuries. Take as many pictures as you can from many different angles. In car accidents, a picture really is worth a thousand words.

Promptly seek medical attention

Go to the emergency room, if necessary, or see your primary care physician as soon as possible after being involved in a motor vehicle accident, regardless of whether you believe your injuries to be serious or minor. Often serious injuries can be masked by the adrenaline from being in an accident, and a comprehensive examination will let you know how you are really doing.

Report the incident to your insurance company

It is not necessary to call your insurance company from the scene of the accident, but many insurance companies do require that you report an accident promptly. If you call the insurance company before consulting with an attorney, you should only give the basic information about how the accident happened. If the insurance company wants more details or to record your call, you should meet with an attorney before going any further.

Contact an attorney

When you contact an experienced attorney, he or she will advocate for you in discussions with insurance companies. Don't give a statement to any insurance company without an experienced attorney at your side. Insurance companies will prevent you from making a full recovery if you do or say the wrong thing.

Contact information of the at fault party:

Name:

Address:

Phone:

Vehicle information of the at fault party:

Make:

Model:

Year:

License plate #:

Insurance information of the at fault party:

Company name:

Policy Number:

Information from responding officer:

Name:

Agency:

Contact information from witnesses:

Name:

Address:

Phone:

Name:

Address:

Phone:

Name:

Address:

Phone:

---

520 Pike Street | Suite 1425 | Seattle, WA 98101 | Tel: 206/720-1501 | Fax: 206/973-1783 www.dubinlawoffice.com

A referral is our greatest compliment. If you know someone in need of our services, please let us know.

279

LAW OFFICES OF
MATTHEW D. DUBIN

THE DUBIN DIFFERENCE

Initial Meeting

- We listen to your concerns
- We explain what we do
- We answer ALL of your questions
- We get basic information about
  - You
  - Your injuries
  - Your treatment
  - Your insurance

Protective bubble

- We deal with any problems or issues that come up
- If you get a bill, letter or phone call, send them to us
- You don't have to talk to anyone but us
- Your only job
  - Get better
  - Get your life back to normal

Information gathering

- Photos
- Witness statements
- Medical records and bills
- Wage loss documentation
- Other expenses
- How your life was affected

Demand/ Negotiation

- Hard-hitting, professional package
- Communicates how your life has been affected
- Documents every penny you are entitled to under the law
- Lets the insurance company know we mean business

Litigation

- Last resort
- Forces insurance company to take your claim seriously
- We continue to negotiate until the end of trial
- We try cases ourselves and work with top litigation specialists to get you results

Life-long relationship

- We want to be your family lawyers
  - If you have a problem we can't handle, we can find you the right lawyer
- We are committed to earning a positive review/testimonial in every case
- Your referral of friends and family to us is the greatest compliment we can earn

www.dubinlawoffice.com

(206) 720-1501

BOOK MATTHEW D. DUBIN
TO SPEAK AT YOUR NEXT EVENT

When it comes to choosing a professional speaker for your next event, you will find no one more respected or successful—no one who can get your audience more excited about optimizing their insurance coverage and protecting their families from the potentially devastating effects of an injury—than Matthew D. Dubin, one of the most knowledgeable personal injury attorneys of our generation.

Whether your audience is 10 or 10,000, in North America or abroad, Matthew D. Dubin can deliver a customized message of hope and inspiration for your meeting, conference, or organization. Matthew understands that your audience does not want to be "lectured," but is rather interested in hearing stories of inspiration, and of real-life people overcoming great odds to maximize their injury claims and protect themselves and their families.

As a result, Matthew D. Dubin's speaking philosophy is to humor, entertain, and inspire your audience with passion and stories proven to move people to take the steps necessary to make sure their families will be safe after a serious injury. If you are looking for a memorable speaker who will leave your audience wanting more, book Matthew D. Dubin today.

To find out whether Matthew D. Dubin is available for your next meeting, contact him by phone or email to schedule a complimentary pre-speech phone interview.

www.dubinlawoffice.com

matt@dubinlawoffice.com

(206) 720-1501